IN MY HEAD
FROM PILOT TO PRISON CAMPS

PEGGIE SINDERS

INSPIRED BY THE LIFE OF THANH CHAU

LUCIDBOOKS

In My Head
From Pilot to Prison Camps
Copyright © 2017 by Peggie Sinders

Published by Lucid Books in Houston, TX.
www.LucidBooksPublishing.com

ISBN-10: 1-63296-146-6
ISBN-13: 978-1-63296-146-4
eISBN-10: 1-63296-169-5
eISBN-13: 978-1-63296-169-3

Special Sales: Most Lucid Books titles are available in special quantity discounts. Custom imprinting or excerpting can also be done to fit special needs. Contact Lucid Books at info@lucidbookspublishing.com.

*Dedicated to all of the South Vietnamese/American troops
who were put in prison camps*

TABLE OF CONTENTS

Foreword   vii

Chapter One: Prison Years, 1975   1

Chapter Two: Training Years   11

Chapter Three: The Beginning of Prison, 1975   15

Chapter Four: Prison Years   47

Chapter Five: Released from Prison, 1984, Age 42   71

Acknowledgments   81

ℱOREWORD

In 1975, I became a VIPS (Volunteers in Public Schools) in an elementary school that had just opened in our new subdivision. For the next 31 years I had the pleasure of being at Kennedy Elementary two days a week. I had many duties, but the one I really enjoyed was working right along with ESL (English as a Second Language) teachers.

In the 1980s, we began seeing many Vietnamese students enrolling in these classes. They were, for the most part, very bright and eager to learn the English language. Little by little, we learned about the hardships these children had encountered in coming to our country.

I, like so many other Americans, had no idea of what had gone on in South Vietnam after our troops were withdrawn in 1973. We were so thankful that our troops were back from so many years of fighting; and after losing so many of our brave men, all that mattered to us was that our soldiers were home. In the years to come, though, I would learn that the South Vietnamese who fought right along with the American troops were captured and were put in communist prison camps soon after the war ended. These prisoners were some of the brightest and most educated men in South Vietnam. The higher in rank, the longer they stayed to live a life of starvation and sickness. They worked daily under some of the worst conditions, building their own huts and working in vegetable gardens, but they were not allowed to eat or enjoy the fruits of their labor.

Four and a half years ago, I met a wonderful man who had been captured and had spent ten long years under the control of the Vietcong in the prison camps. His name is Thanh Chau, and he was a Major in the Vietnamese Air Force in South Vietnam.

This is the true story of Thanh Chau, who braved starvation and so much more. Because Thanh and his fellow prisoners were not allowed to talk with other prisoners, I decided to name this book *In My Head*. Everything was kept in his head, and no other name would fit more perfectly

CHAPTER ONE

Prison Years, 1975

How long have I been asleep? I don't remember ever going to sleep. What is happening to me? My head is throbbing. I can't move. I can't feel my feet. Someone is coughing. I hear moaning. Where am I? I slowly open my eyes. There are bare feet stuck to the side of my face. I need to relieve myself, but I hold it in. A horrible dread encompasses me. I need to move around. I am so very tired and hot. My mouth is dry, and I desperately need a cool drink. I can't turn right or left.

Suddenly I feel something warm where my legs should be. Maybe it's a rat! Oh God, don't let it gnaw on me. Then I notice I have wet myself. Now I know how a caged animal feels. This is what I remember of my first morning in prison.

The year is 1975 and I am 33 years old.

Early Years

I was born in a small town called Baclieu, in South Vietnam, on September 4, 1942. I was named Thanh Chau. I was the second child born to a poor, but hard-working, family. A midwife delivered me as well as my older sister. My mother stayed home to raise her growing family, and my father worked for the French government because at this time we were under the rule of France. Because we were poor, many times we had very little to eat. When I started to school, I wore short pants because we had no money to purchase school clothing.

Some of the children made fun of my pants, but I didn't let it bother me too much because I was a good student and I loved learning many new and exciting things.

In no time at all, we were a family of five children. We played together and we got along well. I can never remember a time that we didn't want to please our parents, and we did everything we could to make them proud of us. If one of us disobeyed in the least, the look on their faces told us how disappointed they were; I think this caused us to be aware of wanting to please them.

In the rainy season in South Vietnam, the weather at night would get very chilly. My mother would wrap us up in mosquito netting because we had no blankets to keep us warm. It was a constant struggle to put food on the table. Our mother would divide her own food with us, her children, and then she would tell us she was not hungry.

We knew at an early age this wasn't always the truth. She was a good mother and I have fond memories of her and of my father. When I was 12, my father decided to move us to Saigon so he could find a better job to support us. He became a merchant and sold just about everything. We pulled together to make our lives somewhat better. My sister, brothers, and I were taught to be the very best in everything that we did. We all made good marks in school and each one of us excelled. Since we were under the rule of France, we were taught French in school. We could all speak it very well, but at home, we spoke Vietnamese.

As I progressed in school, I liked playing sports, especially basketball and soccer. One day I had a chance to play table tennis and soon thereafter it became my favorite sport. I could beat anyone who wanted to play against me. Eventually, I became known in my neighborhood as the little boy who could not be defeated! Oh, how I loved this game! When I completed fifth grade, I started my higher education. I continued to love learning and I was an exceptionally smart student in all of my subjects. At the end of my senior year of high school, I had a big decision to make: I had to choose what I wanted to do with the rest of my life. I decided to join the military in some capacity. I finally chose the Air Force. When I was younger, I had seen planes flying overhead that would drop out papers about airplanes. These leaflets were thrown down to get young boys interested in the Air Force. I became fascinated with them. I knew I would be furthering my education, and I was happy about my decision. I filled out the proper papers for my application. I was one of 1,500 young men who had applied that year. At last I learned that I was accepted because of my good marks. I was ready to begin this new adventure, which would turn out to be the worst and best decision I would ever make in my life.

Training in the Air Force, 1963

We took our basic training at Nha Trang AFB in South Vietnam. For those 1,500 who applied for the Air Force, only 150 men were accepted. I was ready to begin whatever it took to be the best recruit I could be. I knew I was smart, physically fit, and level headed, and I felt I could do most anything I was asked to do.

We completed our basic training in two and a half months, and during that time, the United States sent word to our government that some of the best recruits would be allowed to go to the United States for air cadet training. One hundred fifty of us took the tests that would require us to get the chance to go. I was one of 31 who had passed all of the requirements. What an honor! M.A.P. (Military Assurance Program) would pay for our trip, plus all expenses.

I was on my way! I was so excited to get this offer of a lifetime. I knew some things about America but I never dreamed I would get a chance to go there!

On March 3, 1963, I was 20 years old and well on my way to fulfilling a dream.

While in the States, we would learn the English language and then afterward we would learn all of the names of the planes and functions; finally we would get to fly! We were told we would be learning all of this in Texas.

When we were ready to leave, my heart was beating so fast and I had butterflies in my stomach. This was to be my first time on a plane and the excitement was almost too much! My parents were so proud of me. My sister and brothers told me to take care of myself. My mother and father told me to be respectful to the Americans. We boarded the plane for our long flight that was to take me far away from what I had ever known, to a destination that I knew would be a dream come true.

It was a long and tiring flight, with several stops along the way to change planes. It took 19 hours in all, with very little sleep, to complete our journey. Finally, we arrived at Lackland Air Force Base in San Antonio, Texas. An officer met our plane, and as I walked down the ramp I couldn't believe my eyes—we were actually in the United States! The first thing I noticed about Texas was its spaciousness. The officer put our luggage in a blue van and off we went to the officers' quarters.

Because of our limited English, we used a lot of hand signals, bowing, and smiles. He drove us to our quarters and he took us to our rooms. Before we had a chance to put our belongings away, he told us that dinner was being served. We quickly washed up and joined the other officers that were already in line to eat. We had never seen so much food and so many choices! We watched the other men in front of us and picked out everything they did. We ended up with huge steaks that were as big as the plate, baked potatoes, salad, hot buttered rolls, green beans, chocolate cake, and iced tea. I had never had this much food to eat at one meal! We sat down to eat and everyone was so friendly and helpful to us. We couldn't understand what they were saying but we could tell they wanted us to feel welcome. When we finished eating, we carried our trays to the garbage cans and emptied them. The can was full of leftover food and there was enough to feed a large family for many days from my country.

After dinner, we walked back to our quarters to unpack and get ready for bed. We were so tired, but our stomachs were full from the wonderful meal that we had enjoyed. It didn't take long before we were in our beds, fast asleep.

It seemed as if we had just fallen asleep when it was time to get up and begin our first day of school. We were so excited! After a shower and shave, we walked back to the dining hall for breakfast. I couldn't fathom eating again! I was still full from the night before. There were eggs prepared any way we wanted, bacon, fried potatoes, biscuits, hotcakes, toast, cereal of all kinds, milk, juice, and plenty of hot coffee. I finally decided on eggs, toast, and coffee.

I kept thinking, America is the land of plenty. I had heard this at some time earlier in my life and now I was enjoying the benefits of it!

When we finished breakfast, we began looking over our printed agenda. We were to go to a certain building for ESL classes. One of my buddies found the building, and we walked inside. It was filling up fast. There were long desks and chairs around the room, and my buddies and I found seats near the front and sat down. There were special notebooks, pens, and books on each desk. I looked around and I noticed several other men in uniform from other countries taking this course with us. There were probably 20 to 30 men, altogether.

We later learned there were other rooms where students were learning English. What an opportunity for us to be given such a gift. America was so free and wonderful, and I couldn't help but smile. I knew that when I'd completed my training, at some point I would finally be able to help fight the Vietcong to help stop communism that was threatening my country.

We had several instructors. They were very clear in speaking to us. During our English classes, we learned conversational English. Some of the first things we learned were:

"Yes, I have a pen."

"How are you?"

"Where are you from?"

"I am well, thank you."

"I am from Vietnam."

We had a break for lunch, and then we went right back to class. My buddies and I did very well. We left that afternoon feeling very good about ourselves or, should I say, we felt too good about ourselves!

After dinner, we sat around trying to speak English. I remember very well when one of the American officers walked by and began laughing at us. We couldn't imagine why he was so amused. Later on, we found out that one of us had asked, "How are you?" and another one of us had answered, "Yes, I have a pen." I guess we didn't know as much as we thought!

As the weeks flew by, our ESL classes became much more difficult. Oftentimes, the instructor would sit among us and interact with us individually. He could tell who was learning and what level we were on.

I'm proud to say I mastered each level! My parents would be so proud! I had very good news to tell them in my next letter.

Around the third week, one of the American officers asked me if I would like to go into town to see a movie. I had to tell him no because I had no money. What I had left over, after purchasing the few items I needed for myself, I sent back home to my parents. Many times, I stayed on the base by myself while others went out for fun. The only time I left the base was if it didn't cost anything.

Because there were 31 of us from Vietnam who came to the States, we were divided into different groups. The group I was with became very close and we looked out for one another. I rarely saw the others, but I hoped they did well.

My group progressed with learning the language, and I'm proud to say we all passed! Now we were ready to begin the second stage of our training. We had to learn the names of the planes and the technical names of the parts of the plane and each function. We did some of our study in the classroom and some of our study outside with the planes.

The instructors were equally as friendly as our ESL teachers. They too were well qualified to do their jobs. This course was a challenge. We studied together in my group and we were optimistic that we would eventually become pilots. Even at the beginning of these classes, we knew we had our work cut out for us. The homework was difficult.

I really did have to buckle down on my studies, but I had no doubts about my learning the technical names. I was happy about my determination, which had been instilled in me from my parents, to always do the very best that I could on anything that I did.

While I was at Lackland, I became friends with one of the men who worked there. He and his wife lived in town in a little apartment. He asked me to their home several times, where he did steaks on the grill. Once they took me to a rodeo. This was my first time seeing real cowboys! He found out that I liked to play table tennis, and so did he. He didn't know it at the time but this was my game! As many times as we played, he could never defeat me. Any time that I had free I would be playing table tennis. There were several who thought they could easily beat me but, just like in Vietnam, none could. I was always proud that I was a good player.

While at Lackland, some of the airmen told me about a table tennis competition being held. Everyone thought I should register to compete. What did I have to lose? I thought it would be fun. I would be playing against some of the top players from all over the Southwest, so I registered. I have always been a competitive person by nature and I wasn't nervous about it at all. When the tournament ended, I was the winner! I won a large trophy that was inscribed with Southwest Table Tennis Championship 1963. This was a very rewarding experience for me. I was very pleased with myself. I couldn't wait to write to my family to let them know what I had done.

At the end of our six months at Lackland, we were given orders to move on to Randolph Air Force Base, which was still in San Antonio. Of the 31 from my country to come to the States for training, only 10 completed all of the requirements to move forward. We had succeeded in learning all about the planes, the names of each one, and the function of each part. It had been a wonderful experience during all of our training. Our English was very good at this time and we were ready to move forward. On September 19, 1963, we arrived at Randolph Air Force Base. The airmen here were very friendly and I felt very comfortable with everyone. I still could not get over all of the abundance of food and the variety each time we sat down to eat!

Since we were still in San Antonio, Texas, it wasn't a great deal of difference from being at Lackland. The difference was that I would be getting some hours of flying time. The first plane I flew was the T-28, which was a propeller type. On the first day, I sat in the cockpit with an instructor behind me. I was very nervous but I thought it was to be expected. As I began to gain altitude, I threw up my breakfast. I was deeply embarrassed. The instructor told me not to be worried because it happened all the time. When we landed, I had to fill out a yellow slip of paper and take it to the doctor on base. The doctor asked me many questions, and one of them was if I was homesick for my family. He seemed to think I vomited because I missed my family. He didn't seem to understand that the high altitude caused me to throw up. I'm sorry to say that this happened to me three more times. I only hoped that the same doctor would not be on call each time I went back in! I finally became adjusted and was at ease from then on.

It was such a thrill for me while I was flying, and I knew without a doubt that this was where I belonged.

The second plane I flew was the C-47, a cargo plane with a two-engine propeller used to transport troops. With this particular plane, I had 50 hours of flying time, and with the T-28 I flew 200 hours.

At Randolph, I had learned everything I was trained to do with each plane. I spent most of my time there getting in flying time. I did, however, spend any free time that I had playing table tennis. Everyone there was so friendly and kind.

After 14 months, it was time for me and my buddies to leave Randolph and Texas to fly back to Vietnam. It was November of 1964. Besides leaving with my trophy that I had won at Lackland, I would leave with my two certificates from learning the English language and completing my training in learning all of the names of the planes and each function. I was now an Air Cadet.

I knew I would leave with sad and happy feelings—sad to leave a place where I learned so much knowledge, and happy to get to see my family when I returned.

Back at home, my country was in full-blown war against communist North Vietnam. My buddies and I were anxious to get back, not only to make sure our families were safe, but to use our experience and training. I wanted so badly to help keep my country safe.

When we landed in South Vietnam, I was transferred to Bien Hoa, where I met with my superiors at the headquarters and was briefed. After the briefing, I was allowed to spend a while with my family before I began my duties at the base.

My family was safe and sound, and this made me very happy. They couldn't get over how much I had changed. I knew I had gained a few extra pounds, but I had no idea it would change my appearance. My mother kept pinching my cheeks. I told her it was from all the good food that I had eaten in the United States.

When I returned to the base, I learned that I would be learning to fly the A-1 Skyraider from the US Navy pilots. I spent three months flying with 40 hours flying time. I was so thankful for the Navy pilots who trained me. Now I was much more prepared to help win the war against the Vietcong. I was Second Lieutenant at this time.

In March 1965, President Johnson of the United States sent the first American troops to Vietnam to help fight the North Vietnamese. We were so happy to have them help us. Now we felt sure that we could keep the communists from invading our country. We were thrilled beyond words!

From Bien Hoa, I went to 520 Squadron in order to fly combat missions. I was stationed there for one-and-a-half years. I saw so much bloodshed, not only from the South Vietnamese but also from the American troops. What a miserable life to live. I kept on flying missions day after day trying to eradicate the enemy. I left there in June 1966, to go to Can Tho until 1968. At this time I realized that death was all around us.

We had a mission to do, and we kept on flying and dropping bombs trying desperately to win the war. I felt so bad for the American troops who worked so hard in trying to help us out. The war seemed to never let up. The Vietcong were a vicious people and kept coming after us.

I was ordered back to the United States to learn to fly the A-37. I was soon promoted to First Lieutenant and once again I was stationed at Lackland AFB in San Antonio, Texas. I left Lackland in July 1968—as soon as I'd mastered the A-37—to go fly jet planes at England AFB in Louisiana. I stayed in Louisiana for four months. I desperately needed to fly back to Vietnam where I was promoted to Captain. I was 26 years old. The fighting did not let up. In December 1968, I continued to fly—dropping bombs with 2,500 combat missions all over the enemy territory. It seemed like I was airborne more than I was on the ground, but it wasn't just me fighting. All of my buddies and the American troops were trying to defeat the enemy too. More and more troops were being killed daily. It was such a sad waste to hear of so many losing their lives. The North Vietnamese kept on coming. We were all so very tired and had not much time to rest. Adrenaline kept us going. We kept getting reports of so many deaths and this angered us so much that it caused us to fight even more.

My schedule never differed. It was eat, sleep, and drop more bombs on the enemy. Before long, a year had passed and then another. There were times that I felt like we were making progress. I don't know what we would have done without the troops from the US. They fought so diligently to help us try to control this horrible war.

I had a few days off in 1969. At this time I was to meet the girl of my dreams. Her name was Lien. My parents knew her parents and decided it was time for me to settle down and find someone to share my life. It was an arranged marriage. I had seen this girl on a couple of occasions. I never thought she would eventually become my wife. We dated for six months and afterward I asked her to marry me. When she said, "Yes," I gave her a simple inexpensive ring because I didn't have the money to buy anything else.

I was stationed at Binh Thuy AFB, and during our entire courtship I was very busy dropping bombs. We saw each other when it was possible. It was difficult to set a wedding date. We got word that all around the countryside, people were starving. There were no jobs. Everything was very tense. It seemed as if the war was never going to end.

Finally we set the date for January 2, 1970. We married in her hometown of Can Tho in South Vietnam. I was 28. All of my squadron was there to support me. Lien took my breath away. I never knew I would be so lucky to have such a pretty wife as she. We spent our honeymoon in a beautiful place called Da Lat, high up in the upper region of South Vietnam. Most of the people who lived there were high class French. We stayed one week. It was truly unlike any place I had ever stayed in—such gorgeous scenery.

When our week was over, I had to get back to fighting the war. Nothing had changed back home. It was easy to forget the war while we were away, but now reality was to meet me head on. Lien went back to her home with her parents, and I went back to the Binh Thuy base. I continued to drop bombs.

Before long, another year had passed. We were now parents of a sweet little boy that we named Hieu. I would have loved to have been able to stay at home and be with my family, but the war needed me and my sweet Lien understood. I loved my wife and son so much and it was difficult to leave them each morning. We lived with Lien's parents, and I was at the base when I wasn't dropping bombs. The war seemed as if it were going to last forever.

CHAPTER TWO

*T*RAINING *Y*EARS

On January 1, 1972, I was promoted to Major. I was thrilled beyond words! I knew I would have even more responsibilities, but I didn't mind. I so wanted to help win this long and exhausting war.

Three months after my promotion, we had our second baby—a beautiful little girl that we named Thao. She was healthy and we were proud of her.

On April 30, 1972, President Richard Nixon had all American troops withdrawn from Vietnam. It was a sad time for us, but I knew the troops would not be with us forever. They came over to help us, but not to win the war for us. I knew the Americans were happy to have their troops back home. I felt that we could continue fighting the Vietcong and eventually end the war.

In July 1972, I received orders to go back to Sheppard Air Base in Wichita Falls, Texas. This was my third time in returning there, and another officer would be traveling with me.

When we arrived, I was advised to go to a special meeting where I learned that my assignment would be to oversee the Vietnamese cadets who were there for special training. I was selected to be a Liaison Officer, and my duties were to report to Washington to discuss any problems with the cadets so that any problems could be corrected. What an honor this was for me! I was told that I was selected because of my outstanding abilities and my excellent record. I would be with the cadets most of the time. They were a good group of men and we got along well. I was happy to be able to help them with any concerns and just knowing that I had the backup in Washington to help me made my new title as a Liaison Officer that much more helpful.

The months passed quickly, and toward the end of my year there I was told to go to another meeting. I received a Medal for Distinguished Service for fulfilling my duties as a Liaison Officer. What an honor for me! I was very surprised when the medal was pinned on me. My family would be so happy!

At the end of my duties at Sheppard, three other officers and I were asked to go to Washington, D.C., for one week.

In July 1973, we boarded a plane to Washington. When we arrived, an officer met our plane and drove us to our hotel where we would stay for the duration of our trip.

We found Washington to be very beautiful. The day after we arrived, we received word that we were invited to a dinner, in our honor, at the home of Three-Star General Landal and his wife. The same officer was sent to our hotel to pick the four of us up.

The home was overlooking the Potomac River. It was such a beautiful home and so spacious! The grounds were as lovely as the home. The General opened the door and invited us inside. His wife, a Filipino lady, greeted us warmly. We were introduced and told to walk to the dining room. A table was set with beautiful china, and candles were lit to make the table more welcoming. We enjoyed a delicious meal.

General Landal told us, during the course of the meal, that he had been to South Vietnam as an advisor. While there, he met with First President Ngo Dinh Diem. The General said he held the Vietnamese people in high regard. At one point, he asked me if I had ever entertained the idea of living in the United States. This question took me by surprise! I finally told him, "No, because I have my wife and family back in Vietnam." He smiled at me as if to say, "You need to think about it!"

After dinner, we were told to go to the living room. There was a large piano, and the General walked over to it and began to play. He asked us to join him. We stood around and he began to play songs that we vaguely remembered hearing on the radio during our trips to the US. We all sang as best as we could. At one point, the General recorded our voices.

The evening ended with strong handshakes and pats on the back. We told them how much we enjoyed our visit and the dinner. The officer with the van drove up and we went back to the hotel. The four of us agreed that this particular evening would never leave our memories. At our hotel, the officer told us that he would be back to pick us up the next morning to take us sightseeing, that is, if we wanted to go. Of course we all said, "Yes!"

The next morning, we were dressed and very excited when the officer drove up. We spent the entire day visiting so many places. We saw the Lincoln Memorial and Capitol Hill, as well as others. At one point, we got out of the van and walked around. Over a period of four days, we saw numerous sights. We went to the Pentagon. It was a huge complex that served as Headquarters of the US Department of Defense. It employed so many people. There were many parts that we were blocked from visiting. This was understandable to us. During the time that we were in Washington, I couldn't help but think about my country that was in a full-blown war, yet here I was sightseeing and having a good time. I felt I needed to be dropping bombs instead. I was honored to have this opportunity and to have been asked to come, but I couldn't help but have these feelings.

My week of spending time in this beautiful place was soon up. The officer picked me up at the hotel to drive me to the airport. I thanked him for taking me all over Washington. The officer who traveled to Washington with me would follow later on after he had completed his assignment. I was more than anxious to get back to dropping bombs.

When I arrived back in Vietnam, I went back to the base at Binh Thuy. I was briefed, then soon after, I was back dropping bombs—just like I was before I left for the United States.

I went back home to see my wife and family. I was anxious to see if they were all safe and sound. I was thankful that everyone was well and they were so happy to see me.

Each day fighting the Vietcong was tiring, but I felt we were able to do our jobs well. I was confident that we would win this horrible war.

Day after day, I saw so many of our men get killed and this was so hard to get through daily. I was positive that we would be able to keep the enemy at bay. Months went by, and soon we were in our third year of fighting without the American troops.

It soon became apparent to us that our supplies were getting low. I couldn't help but think that we could win this war if we had supplies coming in.

On April 30, 1975, the war finally ended. The Vietcong took complete control of my country. What a sad and pitiful day for all of us. How downhearted we all felt. We lost the war because of one reason only. We ran out of supplies. Back at our base, we were told to go home and stay there.

It is estimated that two million South Vietnamese were killed, three million were wounded, and another 300,000 became refugees.

CHAPTER THREE

THE BEGINNING OF PRISON, 1975

I have vivid pictures in my mind of the day my life changed so drastically. It was a warm day in April. I was at home with my family. Our two children, Hieu, who was five and Thao, age three, had just finished their lunch and were napping. My wife, Lien, who was five months pregnant with our third baby, was cleaning the dishes.

Suddenly, I heard a loud commotion coming from outside. I quickly ran up the stairs to look over the balcony, and I saw three men with machine guns. They began shouting for me to come out! Before I had a chance to turn around, the men stormed inside our home, running up the stairs screaming for me to surrender. I actually thought they were going to kill me! They kept screaming for me to put my arms above my head. They told me to freeze and if I moved they would shoot me! The look on my wife's face will forever be etched in my mind as they shoved me out the door to the waiting truck.

Beginning of Prison

Inside the truck, I was terrified and I kept wondering how this ordeal was going to affect my family emotionally. I had no idea where they were taking me. It didn't look good, no matter where it was. I made myself sit still and I looked straight ahead. Out of the corner on my eye I glimpsed the men. They were not men at all. They were only boys trying to act tough. They could not have been more than 17 or 18 at most. Oh, how I wished I was back home with my family.

Just yesterday, I was at Bien Hoa Air Force Base where I was stationed as a Major and our commanding officer informed us that South Vietnam had been taken over by North Vietnam. He ordered us to go home and stay inside.

Our country had been taken over by the Vietcong. Everything that was ours was all lost. What a heartbreaking feeling to know that all of this was happening and I was in the middle of it all.

Finally, we drove up to what was once the old police station where hardened criminals were once kept. They shoved me out of the truck while pointing their machine guns at me. We walked inside and I saw approximately 60 to 70 other officers already there. We were searched and they took everything from us except the clothes we were wearing. They continued to shout at us. They did not want us talking to each other. I looked around and I saw some of the officers that I knew personally. Everyone I saw were the top-echelon, high in rank, and educated South Vietnamese being interrogated by a bunch of Vietcong with machine guns. We made gestures with our eyes to each other; occasionally someone would whisper to another. There was no way we could talk without the guards hearing us. There was so much we wanted to say. I continued looking at the officers. We were all astonished to know we were here together.

By now it was late evening and we were so tired and hot. I continued to give no eye contact with the guards. They were strutting in and around us making sure we saw their guns. One of the guards was having trouble holding his because the gun seemed bigger than he was. I would have laughed had I not been so scared. The room soon become unbearable because we were so crowded together. Other guards brought in small plates of rice and chunks of monias—which is similar to a sweet potato, only they are not sweet. I saw that the plates were crusted with dried food and what little food there was looked nasty. There were small rocks mixed into the dirty rice. Occasionally I could hear the men scraping the rocks to the side of their plate. I hoped and prayed that we would soon be able to go back to our families. I was wrong.

After we ate, the guards told us to lie down all around the perimeter of the room. There were platforms built, which were made of concrete for us to sleep on. The guards shouted for us to sleep feet to face; in other words we could not face each other. I suppose this was to keep us from talking to each other. Several needed to relieve themselves and they were taken out, a few at a time, with the ever present guns always pointed at them. The guards passed out thin mats for us to sleep on. Oh, how hard the platforms were, and most of us did not sleep very well.

The next day, we were ordered to stand up. My back hurt so much, and I am sure the other officers felt the same as me. We were once again given the same miserable meal served on the same dirty dishes. We ate because we were hungry. Before long, the shouting began for us to be quiet. We were ordered to go outside in single file to exercise. We stayed out for about an hour before we were ordered back inside.

On day four, we were ordered to get up much earlier than usual. We were stiff from sleeping on a hard floor. When I tried to get up, again I found it to be of great difficulty. My back hurt something terrible. I was afraid one of the guards would kick me—or far worse. I finally stood up. We again ate the awful food served on the same filthy plates. Afterwards, we were told to walk single file out of the building to waiting trucks. Oh, how I wished we would be going home.

After riding for a good amount of time, we reached our destination. It was the military officers' prison—it wasn't the home I am sure everyone was hoping for. There were several barracks built around a compound. We were shown a tub in the back of the building that had running cold water where we could wash ourselves once a day if we were good prisoners. We were also told to dig a large hole on the side of the barracks, which was to be our latrine. We were issued hoes and shovels to dig with. After the task was completed, we were given a drink of dirty-looking water. I could hear gagging. We all drank very fast because we were so hot and thirsty. We soon had bloated stomachs. How angry I was. I began thinking about our ordeal. We had done nothing wrong. Our only reason was that we were South Vietnamese officers. We had worked so hard to become officers, and with all of our special training and education, why were we ending up this way? This is not the way any of us envisioned our lives to be.

I began thinking of my family. How were they doing? My sweet children, Hieu and Thoa, and my beautiful wife. How was she doing? We had a new baby coming in a few months.

On our third day here, one of the guards stood in front of me. What could he want of me? I had done everything that they had told me to do. I actually thought he was going to shoot me. We had been outside exercising at the time. He ordered me inside the building. He told me I had a visitor. He told me to stand behind a wall with a small window.

All at once, I saw my beautiful wife! She was with my father-in-law. There was so much I wanted to say. The guard told us we had 10 minutes. He pointed the gun toward the floor. There were tears in Lien's eyes. I wanted so much to touch her but because of the partition between us, I could only look at her. She asked me how I was. I opened my mouth but no words came. Everything was stuck in my throat. She told me she had brought a package with some food and other things that I probably needed. I remembered thanking my father-in-law for bringing her to me. I also remember mumbling my words to her. I hoped she would understand that because we were ordered to not talk to the other prisoners for so long that maybe I had forgotten how to talk. She looked so sweet, and I also noticed she looked very healthy and had been taking care of herself and the baby that soon would be delivered. Not long after, the guards said that our time was up. I wanted her to stay so that I could just look at her. She and her father walked away. I wanted so much to scream for her to come back. The guards motioned for me to go back outside. I began to think how miserable I must have looked to her. I had lost weight and I was filthy with sweat.

I still had on the same clothes that I was captured in, but I had seen my wife, and this was a special time for me. That evening, when our meal was served, one of the guards brought me the package that Lien had brought. I could tell right away that the box had been opened and the guards had most likely taken out some of the things inside for themselves. Not only was there some food, there were also several toiletries. I shared the food with some of the other officers around me. The food tasted so delicious. It had been so long since we'd had anything so good.

At bedtime, I lay on my bunk thinking about our ordeal. I wondered how long we would be here. I most likely wouldn't be home in time to be with Lien when she delivered our new baby. It had been so wonderful seeing my wife, but it wasn't long enough to be with her.

I began to be very depressed. I had to struggle with myself to make something positive of the day. I made a promise right then to not let the Vietcong get the better of me. I would be an example to the other men. Earlier in my training days, I had become a Liaison Officer. I could do this! I would keep my composure. I thought of the other officers. I knew they were scared, angry, and hungry. They all wanted to go home. I wanted to go home as well.

My parents came to visit me. They looked so old. I knew they were worried sick about me. My father asked me if I were being treated well. I lied and told him yes. My mother could not talk. She only cried.

The next day, we were ordered to go outside in single file. As long as we were here, we had to keep the grounds clean. We were given hoes, rakes, and shovels to do the work. Every day, we worked out in the stifling heat—only stopping once in a while to have a drink of the warm dirty-looking water. The only way I could drink it was to pretend it was clean.

The hole we had dug earlier for our latrine had become almost unbearable to use. The smell was something awful. The waste inside was rotting in the hot sun. Flies were always buzzing around.

Sometimes they would fly into our mouths. In the middle of all of this mess, maggots were squirming about. The guards could have easily poured something in it to keep the smell down. This was just one more thing we had to endure.

More and more men were becoming sick with diarrhea. The guards passed out local medication. I did not accept any. For all I knew, it could be poison. It did seem to help some of the prisoners, but I would take my chances.

If I wasn't thinking of my family, I was thinking of food. Oh, how wonderful it would be to have fresh fruit or just good, clean food.

At night, as I lay on my bunk, I would become so angry. Sometimes I would drift off to sleep only to have a bad dream. I always felt confined and choking. I would wake up drenched in sweat. Occasionally, I would hear someone softly moaning. How long were we to endure this kind of life? What was its purpose? Sometimes I would tell myself to bear with it. Tomorrow would be a better day. I knew in my heart that it would not be better, but I would tell myself it would be, anyway.

One day, when I was out chopping down the tall weeds, one of the men began to sway. I quietly walked over to him and with the side of my hip I propped him up long enough for him to regain his strength. I did not know what the guards would do if we could not stand up. I tried not to think about it. I hoped by the afternoon he could go out to the tub and get cooled off and make himself feel better.

I began having more and more nights when I would wake up having had a bad dream. I did not know which was worse, having these dreams or living them.

My parents came again to visit me. I guess my father had talked to my mother before they came because she did not cry, but I cried when they left.

Most of the men were sick with diarrhea. Some of them would not make it to the hole in time before they would make a mess that would run down their legs. Since we were to use the tub only once a day, this made it very difficult for them. Sometimes they would slosh the water from the faucet to wash themselves as quickly as possible, only to mess themselves once again.

Occasionally, we would take off our clothes, wash them with our hands and put them back on—soaking wet. In no time at all, they would be dry. My clothes were so filthy that no amount of washing would clean them. I had a difficult time trying to keep my pants up because of the weight I had lost. What a great feeling it would be to tear off these old clothes and throw them away; then again, by doing this, I would be throwing away the only thing I could call my own.

I do not know the exact date when there was a change of sorts in the prison. Every few days, we would have someone come in to talk to us about communism. They talked to us about how wonderful it would be if we would only accept their way of life. Everything would be perfect. I had seen enough of their perfect way of life and under no circumstances would I ever accept it. Their promises seemed ideal. It sounded too perfect! I don't know if any of the prisoners changed their minds. Maybe a couple of them did. None of the prisoners that I knew did. These talks did not surprise me. In fact, I expected all of their propaganda and it meant nothing to me. Here we were, starving, sick, and sometimes not thinking clearly. This is the way they wanted it. They wanted us to be weak and tell them we were guilty and become one of them. It was difficult to hear all of this nonsense, but most of us sat up listening but not really listening. I tuned it all out and thought about food or my family. I did not want to think about what happened to us if we dozed off. I noticed everyone sat up straight and pretended to listen as if it were the most interesting thing they had ever heard.

We heard these talks often. I wondered sometimes if their way of life was really that great for all of them. I never for a moment thought it was because I could see nothing that would ever make me change my mind.

There were days when I would look over at the other officers. I could see a steady decline in their health. I knew it was from lack of proper nourishment and the filthy conditions we had to live in.

Many times, the men would complain of a headache. Sometimes the guards would hand out local medication and other times they would do nothing at all. For the most part, we learned to suffer through whatever we had. I often would wonder what I looked like since we had no mirrors—but then again, I only had to look at the others to see a reflection of myself. We were a miserable-looking bunch of men. We were all healthy and in good condition when we were captured, but now there was nothing left of our original selves.

One day, the guards decided we needed to have our hair cut and a shave. What a relief! At last we would look somewhat better. Some of us had received razors and scissors from our families but the guards had kept them. We were allowed to do this once every month. The guards would always be standing in and around us in case we wanted to harm them. No matter how much we hated the Vietcong, we would never do harm to them because we knew what they would do to us with their guns that were always pointed at us.

One good thing about us getting a haircut and shave was that we were allowed to shave each other as well as cut each other's hair. During these times, we would mouth to each other something we wanted to say. We had to be very careful and many times one of the guards would walk over and shout in our faces to be quiet.

One day I was called inside the building. This time I wasn't as scared as I was before. I thought perhaps my wife and her father were coming to see me. I stood behind the wall with the window. At once, I saw my beautiful Lien with her father. We went through the same routine with only 10 minutes to talk to each other. She looked so healthy. I tried not to embarrass myself by not talking clearly like I had before. She asked me how I was doing. I told her I was doing well. She could see I was not, but she tried to be upbeat for me. We chatted about the children at home and in no time, our 10 minutes were up. I told them both goodbye. In my heart, I felt so thankful that her father went all this distance to bring my wife to me.

It was getting harder and harder to keep myself sane. We would get up each morning and eat our pitiful meal and walk out to begin clearing the grounds. I had an infection around my finger from the blisters that would get dirt inside and break open. It was difficult for me to use the rakes and hoes.

The nights were the worst thing about being in prison. I was now waking up every night having experienced a bad dream. I again felt confined and choking. Sometimes I would try to stay awake for fear of waking up again moaning and crying loudly. I always woke up with my clothes soaked with sweat. I knew we all feared waking up screaming. We had no idea what the guards would do to us. Then one night, our worst fears became a reality. One of the men must have had such a dream. He woke up screaming. Some of the men sleeping nearby were trying to soothe him. They too were in danger

22

for trying to help. The screaming became louder and louder. Nothing was helping. The guards came rushing over and grabbed his arms and pulled him out. He continued to scream. We all listened. No one made a sound. We waited and waited. We could hear nothing. We were waiting for the sound of a gunshot. We heard nothing except the quietness of our room. In time, we tried to go back to sleep. The next morning, each of us looked over in the direction of where the man had been sleeping. I guess we wanted him to be there with us. He was not. We never found out what happened to him. Thankfully I did not know him. I had heard one of the guards mention his name to another guard as they were talking about him. I could not help thinking about him. He was a human being, an officer, someone's son, someone's father, and someone's brother. He was gone and never coming back. He was killed by one of the animals who controlled our every move.

As each day passed, the more depressed we all became. Oh, how weak we were. It was next to impossible to get up each morning. My skin had turned a sickly color that was almost black. My arms and legs had loose skin hanging off of them. Some of the men were sicker than others, but none of us was well. I had to think of something positive—anything to keep going. I so wanted to be upbeat for the other officers as I looked at them. I still had a strong desire to help the men, but it was becoming more and more difficult. We all smelled. I was always thankful when it was my turn to go to the tub. I knew each of us liked to be as clean as we possibly could.

One day, I began to think about our new baby that was due. We had no way to tell what month it was—much less what day. I knew it must be close to her due date. I wondered what the baby would be. We already had a boy and a girl so it did not make much difference what this one would be. Sadness was taking over my thoughts. I wished I could be there with Lien. Oh, how hard this was on her to not have me there to help with the other children. I wanted to cry from loneliness. I missed my family so much. I tried not to cry very often because it took so much energy from me. Would we ever go home? I could not let my imagination run away with me. I made myself think of family or food—I could have neither. Sometimes I would ask myself what I wanted to eat more than anything. Most of the time I thought about fresh fruit or fresh vegetables.

One day, while outside chopping weeds, I noticed one of the men creeping up on something. Whatever it was, he caught it and quickly put it in his mouth. He saw me looking and opened his mouth so that I could see. It was a grasshopper. I was not shocked. We were all starving. I too was hungry, like the man, but at this particular time I could not eat a grasshopper. Maybe sometime I would try. I turned and began chopping in another direction.

At night, after we had eaten our pitiful meal, we would lie down in our bunks. I knew every man here would be thinking of his family. This particular night, I looked over toward a couple of the men. I began thinking that I had never seen them being called into the building because of a visitor. Maybe their families did not know where they were. Maybe they thought they were dead. I could not imagine not having someone to care about them. Maybe next time Lien brought me a package, I would share some of the food with them.

One of the many chores that we had to do at the compound was to empty the hole at the side of the building. I always hated this. I would have done anything to keep from doing this filthy task. But as usual, we did not have a choice. We would be given buckets to dip the waste and carry it out to an open area and deposit it. Other prisoners would spread ash and dried leaves over the waste. This chore was the most degrading thing we had to do. An hour after emptying the waste, we could still smell the stench in our nostrils. This had to be done many times during the month because there were so many of us using it. This could have been done an easier way if the guards had put something in the hole to keep the smell down, but we never did anything in an easier way. The Vietcong made sure of it.

One day, my jaw started hurting. I could feel my gums swelling in the back of my mouth. It seemed as if my teeth were becoming loose. As the days continued to go by, the swelling increased. I could taste pus and I spit it out constantly. My neck was also swelling. When I put my hand around the area I could feel it was hot. I knew I needed medication to take the infection down but of course there was none. The only thing I could think of was to rinse my mouth with water when I would have a drink. I knew the water was not sanitary and it probably would do more harm than good. I was happy that my wife sent toothpaste and toothbrushes in my packages. I could at least keep my mouth as clean as possible. Finally, the swelling went down and I began to feel a little better. I could not help but wonder what else I would encounter with my health.

One night, I began scratching my arms and legs. There were also huge welts on my stomach. It took a while for it to register in my head that we all had bed bugs in our bunks. Our bedding, what little we had, was never washed and there was no way to get rid of these pests. I had noticed the men had bleeding sores on their legs and arms and now we were infected with another worry to add to our already long list of woes.

My wife and her father came to visit me again. It was always wonderful seeing them. Lien looked as if the baby would be due any day. I always worried about her coming all this distance to see me. As always, she had tears in her eyes, which she tried to conceal from me. I told her she looked well and again I thanked her father for bringing her to me.

There was no way I could ever thank him enough for doing such a brave thing for my wife and me. She asked me how I was doing and I told her I was doing just fine. She could see how I looked. I saw her looking me over and she saw how terrible I looked. My clothes were filthy and I could barely keep my pants up. She could see how much weight I had lost. Time was up and like always, it ended too soon. Before they walked out, she told me that she had brought another package for me. I told them goodbye. She was gone. It was all I could do to keep my composure until I went back outside to work. I picked up my hoe and I let the tears run down my face. How was I ever going to think of something positive to keep me going? One of the guards was looking at me, so I dried my tears and began hoeing.

Late that night, I heard it begin to rain. It had been an unusually hot and muggy day so I knew at once the rainy season was upon us.

It was hard to imagine that we had been in prison for five months. Five long months I had endured being away from my family. I had no idea we had been away this long. I had to remind myself that I would not fall apart. I had made this promise to myself. I had to be strong for the other officers. I couldn't be strong in thinking, the way I was right then. So, once again, I pulled my emotions from somewhere deep inside and I began thinking positively. It was becoming more and more difficult to think of something good. I thought about my family and this seemed to help pull me out of despair—most of the time.

Each day, the rain fell softly and each night, in my bunk, I could hear it beating on the roof. Somehow it was soothing to listen to. We began to have thunder sounding in the distance. I started thinking about our children. They did not like thunder. They would come running to me or Lien for comfort. I wondered if it was storming at home. Were they thinking of me on this particular night? Would Lien be able to soothe the children by herself?

There was not much to do outside the next day because of the rain. Once outside, if the rain became harder we would go inside. I preferred to work, if possible, because it kept my mind from feeling so sad.

One of the men, who had just seen his wife earlier in the day, saw me and mouthed to me, "You had a baby girl and everything is okay, she was born September sixth."

I was overjoyed! She was born so close to my own birthday. I had not thought of my birthday on September fourth. Now tonight I was thirty-four years old. I was the father of three children. I was so sorry I could not have been there with my wife when she needed me the most. I was heartbroken that I was not there to hold this sweet new addition to my family. Tears began to slide down my face. I could not remember feeling so defeated. I lay down in my bunk and it was as if all hope was drained from me. How would I ever be able to feel something good? My thoughts went quickly to the news I heard earlier about our new baby. I began telling myself this was good news! I did not know when it would be, but if I could hold my family in my arms, everything would be all right. It had to be. I could not, nor would I, let myself go down in those dark pits tonight. I put my hand over my heart and I was lulled to sleep by the sound of the rain beating down on the roof.

The next morning, the rain was coming down in sheets and we wouldn't be able to go to work outside. This would be a perfect day for the Vietcong to come in telling us to surrender and join up with them for a better way of life in the communist party. Instead, the guards came in carrying large boxes that they deposited on the floor in front of us.

They told us to line up and grab one of the uniforms inside. We were actually getting new clothes! They told us they were all the same size and to not linger and keep moving on as we picked them up. I picked mine up, walked over to my bunk, and took off the filthy rags I had been wearing since I was first captured. The uniforms were blue with long sleeves, and the pants had a drawstring belt. Now I could move around without the pants falling down. I looked around and everyone had uniforms several sizes too big. There were hints of smiles on each face. This was the first time in over five months that everyone smiled together. I knew the smiles would not last, but for now it was a good feeling to shed the old clothes and be happy in the moment.

Today we had another shave and haircut. We took turns grooming each other. Lice were rampant among the men. Some of them had sores that were bleeding from scratching so much. The guards, like always, were walking in and around us with their guns pointed at us. Most of us were so weak from starvation that we couldn't retaliate even if we wanted too. Most of us had lost some of our hair from poor health and we had only patches here and there on our heads. What a sad-looking group of men we were. Some of the officers had trouble standing for long periods of time because of being so weak.

When nighttime came, we were more than ready for bed. It had been raining really hard all day so we had not gone out to work. When we didn't work it made for a very long day. It was still raining in the evening, but not as much as it had been. There was whispering among some of the officers that one of the officers had decided to make a break for it. I think he was one the men who never got any visitors. Maybe he couldn't stand it any longer and was going home to find out why he never heard from anyone. Sometime during the night, he left by sneaking out quietly when he thought the guards would not be looking.

The next morning, when it was time to get up, we noticed that the officer who left was not back. We thought this was a good sign that he made it out. We all felt optimistic. The guards brought in our little breakfast. We ate and began getting ready to file in line to go out to work. All of a sudden, the men in the front of the line started making a commotion. When I got to the door I saw what they had seen. There, tied to a tree right in front of us, was the officer who had tried to run away. One of the guards shouted to us to stop going any further. We were told not to walk up to the prisoner and not to offer him a drink. We were told not to talk to him or give him eye contact. My heart felt so bad for him. Most of us were in shock. It took every bit of courage that I had to walk out and begin working.

All morning, and all during the day, I could hear the poor man begging for a drink. I noticed some of the officers were working with tears sliding down their faces. I did not cry, not because I couldn't have—oh, yes, I could have cried buckets—but because I was so angry. Oh, how I would have liked to tie every one of the guards up. I would have loved to have been able to kick them until they were a bloody mess. How could any human being be this sadistic? It took the pitiful officer two days to die. Two days of moaning in agony. This kind of happening does something to a man. You want so badly to take revenge. I saw myself untying the officer over and over all day in my mind. I knew I would never get over seeing this horror happening.

Occasionally, planes would fly over the compound where we were. Two days after we arrived here, we had to dig a foxhole for ourselves. The guards did not tell us why, but I knew the Vietcong did not want anyone to know that we were imprisoned out here. It was a back-breaking task because our shovels were dull from using them to dig our latrine. We were ordered to get inside them. Getting inside the foxhole was easy. Getting out of it was difficult. Our bodies were depleted so badly that we had lost all of our muscle tone. We had to use the upper part of our bodies to lift ourselves out. It took every bit of our strength.

After the death of the officer who was tied to the tree, there were days when I could not remember one day to the next. I guess it was nature's way of helping me cope. I went about going through the motions of what we had to do outside. Many days we did not work because of the muddy conditions. This was a very low period for all of us. There seemed to be less and less of me wanting to be helpful to the other men. I could not even help myself.

My wife and her father came to see me again. At the time, we had been ordered into our foxholes. When she walked up with the guard, I was surprised to see her. She had brought our new baby to see me. She bent down to show me Quyen, the name she had picked out for her. The guard let me touch the baby. My hands were filthy from the dirt, but how sweet she felt to me. She looked at me with her big eyes. She had no idea who I was. Would she ever know me? Lien was so proud to show me the baby. They both looked so healthy. I was thankful that they were. It hurt so badly that I could not visit longer with them. There was so much I wanted to say. It seemed as if they had just come and the 10 minutes were up much too soon. I told them goodbye and they were gone.

Later that evening, the guards brought me the box that Lien and her father had brought with them. I divided up the food with my fellow officers who were near me. There was never enough, but what little there was tasted so delicious.

One day, one of the officers passed around a small calendar. I suppose his family sent it in one of his packages. When the calendar came to me, I quickly added up the days and the months. I must have calculated wrong and I again counted up the days. Could it be possible that we had been here for over 10 months? I could not imagine us being here that long. I gave the calendar back to the officer next to me. I felt sick at heart. Would we ever get out? I wished I knew what the plans were for us. Were we doomed to die here? Oh God, I was so lonely for my little family. Would I ever be optimistic again? The day finally ended with my mind feeling so empty. Would my children remember me? Would anyone care? I began thinking of my beautiful Lien. Yes, she cared. She came to see me as often as she could. She certainly would not come if she did not care. These thoughts once again gave me reason to hang on a little longer.

Every few weeks, the guards would change. At first, I thought we would get one or two who would be different and let us talk once in a while or not shout so loudly at us. There was to be no such luck for any of the officers. Every guard we had was exactly like the rest. I thought they probably went to a class where they were taught to be as vicious as possible. There was nothing nice I could ever say about them. Each one did a great job of trying to make us feel as low class as we felt about them.

One morning, we woke up to find one of our officers dead. I suspected he'd died of starvation. I wondered how many more would die the same way. Oh, how I prayed he would be the only one. We all sat around feeling terrible for him. We needed to talk in the worst way so that we would be better with coping with his death. I hated the Vietcong. I wondered if they would bury him in a respectable manner. I doubted it. The poor man was finally out of his misery and he would not suffer anymore.

The days dragged on, one day after another. We had seen so much sadness since we were captured. I did not think it could be any worse. Again, I was wrong. Two more officers died of starvation. I was once again at a low point in my life. It was more difficult this time for me because I had known one of the men.

The days following the death of my friend, I could not stop my tears. I felt as if I could do nothing else. I felt so defeated inside. I had tried so hard to keep myself sane, especially for my fellow officers. I felt I could not go on. I had no desire to try and help anyone. The brainwashing was actually working. I was letting the enemy do to me exactly what they wanted. My inner feelings were gone. All I wanted to do was to lie down and let the Vietcong take me. There seemed nothing left of my spirit.

Just when I felt like giving up, one of the officers walked over to me and began to pat my shoulder. I suppose he had been watching me. This small act of kindness seemed to jar me back to reality. I don't know how this was done to me without the guards seeing but they had not. I wished I could have thanked him. I felt as if everything was going to be all right.

This simple touch did wonders for me. I found out, that evening, how important touching really is. I now felt as if I wasn't the only one trying to keep all of us upbeat. I had made myself feel as if it were.

No, I could not do it alone. We had to pull together in the smallest way and now I felt relief inside. I could still be of help to the others but it would no longer be just me. We were a team here, and as I began to drift off to sleep in my bunk that night, I began thinking how thankful I was that the Vietcong did not have me—and I somehow knew they never would.

My wife and her father came to visit me again. As always, it was wonderful to see them. Lien always asked me how I was. I guess she was just trying to make small talk. She could see that I wasn't feeling well. At this time in prison, I knew I was just a shell of what I used to be. She never told me during our visits but I could tell it was probably very difficult for her to talk to me without falling to pieces. I'm sure her visits must have left her drained. I would never say I didn't enjoy seeing her but I could only imagine how hard it was on her to leave and go back to our children. My wife was a very strong woman. I learned this during her visits to me.

Every once in a while, the little calendar would be passed around. In some ways, it would help to see the dates. My children Hieu and Thao had had birthdays. They were growing each day and changing—as children do. I would wipe away tears just thinking about them. My beautiful wife had also become a year older. Would I ever leave this place and go home? I was so thankful of the times my wife came to see me. It was getting more difficult each time she left. I'm sure each officer here had the same reaction about their families. I found out that my wife and the children were living with her parents. At least they were being taken care of.

Early one morning, as we were eating our little meal, the guards came rushing in to tell us we were leaving. Could we possibly be going home? I tried not to get my hopes up since I had been wrong on so many other occasions. We were ordered to get into formation. We lined up and were ordered to march. It was very hot and I didn't know how long we could march. I know how I felt and I knew the other prisoners were as hot and as tired as I was. Finally we stopped and were given a drink of warm water. We were so thirsty. Again we were told to continue marching. We marched for a couple of hours and were told to stop and have another drink. We continued to march. Oh, God, how many more miles were we to march? I honestly did not think we could continue much longer in our weakened condition.

Finally we reached our destination. We were ordered to stop and were given another drink. As we were drinking our water, we all looked in amazement. We were at the train station. We were not going home. We all looked downcast. Where could we be headed this time? We were not told anything. The only thing we knew for sure was that we would be traveling on a train. We continued to stand, and in our weakened condition it was only a matter of time before we would begin to drop like flies.

The guards began shouting for us to walk toward the cargo section of the train where cattle were transported. We lined up and were shoved inside. We had a hard time getting up into the car, but thankfully we all made it. Once inside, the guards slid the large door shut. It was dark and smelled of cow waste. It was difficult to breathe. Everyone pushed in front of each other to get to the slats to breathe. I began to think there was no way we would make it out alive without clean air. It seemed like forever before the train began to move. Slowly at first, and after a long time, we picked up speed.

For the first time since we had been in prison, there was shouting among us. Everyone wanted to go to the slats to take a large gulp of air. Some did not want to give up their places and there was a lot of shoving and shouting among us.

I decided it was up to me to gain some sense of order among the men. I told the men to stop shouting because we would surely die if we kept it up. We needed to keep ourselves calm and show some self-control. At last everyone quieted down.

We sat on the floor of the filthy car. This way we could let the air flow over us. Much to our surprise, the train began to slow down and finally stopped. We had been on the train about two hours, and since we had no way of knowing where or how long we would be traveling, it would be a relief to finally get out of the hot box.

Even though we had stopped, it seemed like forever before the guards opened the sliding door. We were all completely wet with sweat and I was overjoyed to see that every one of the men in my group had made it out alive. I was thankful that we all had settled down during our ordeal and this had helped us to continue our journey to wherever.

We were all exhausted. It was hard for all of us to get out of the packed train. We were ordered to stand at attention. Finally, we stood but for how long I did not know. We were given a drink of warm water. I told the men to drink slowly so we wouldn't get sick. One of the guards came over and stuck his face into mine and shouted for me to be quiet. I was proud that I had spoken up. It would probably be the last time I would be able to.

After we had all been given a drink of the warm water, we were told to begin marching. I was glad that on the train we were all able to sit down. Maybe we could withstand marching. I only hoped we wouldn't have to go too far. We marched for about two hours before we were told to halt.

Everyone wondered where we were going. In the distance, I could see ships in the water and smaller boats. Where could we possibly be going? Then it dawned on me. We were going to North Vietnam. Oh, God, it could be much worse. The smell of the water and the blue sky would have been a sight to enjoy, but there was no joy from any of the officers. We were so tired. All we could do was look at the water.

We marched closer to one of the old ships that was docked. I looked around. Everywhere I looked I could see other officers from the same camp that we had left hours ago. We had never been able to converse with any of these men. It was good to finally see that we were all together once again. We were ordered to board the cargo ship.

We marched to the ship, going down several winding stairs until we finally reached the very bottom. It never ceased to amaze me how the Vietcong outdid themselves doing the most hideous things to us. We were forced inside where cattle had been transported from one place to another. It was dark and smelled of waste. There was cow poop everywhere. It was difficult to walk about without sliding around in the muck. I was thankful we didn't have far to slide because we were so crowded together. It was so dark and oh, the smell was terrible.

I began thinking about how long we had been in the compound. It had been 14 months. Now we were on our way to somewhere else. How long would we be in prison before we could go home? It had become easy to think we might never get the chance.

The guards threw down a box of dried noodles for us to eat. They closed the hatch and were gone. It soon became almost unbearable to breathe. It was pitch black. There was very little room to move about and oh, how hot it was. I heard some of the men coughing, but none of us said a word. What was there to say? Now that we were alone without the guards shouting at us, no one had any desire to talk. My heart was broken. We were down in the lowest part of the ship. Now we were no better than the cattle that were down here before us. What kind of people were the Vietcong? How much more could we stand?

Our eyes finally became accustomed to the darkness. We could make out those next to us.

The guards lowered down a bucket of water with one small cup for all of us to drink from. There was a rope attached to a pulley that allowed the bucket to be lowered. The water was warm but we all drank it just the same. We could have had more but this was all we had and we had to share it. When the bucket was empty, we attached it to the rope and sent it back up. Later that evening, a larger bucket was lowered down for us to relieve ourselves. As the bucket was being hauled up, it began sloshing out all over us. We tried to wipe ourselves as best as we could with our hands. We soon became filthy from the waste. We were already dirty and our clothes were soaked with sweat. Now we had to endure one more thing.

Someone found the box of dried noodles and passed them around. We began chomping down the tasteless noodles. This was to be our evening meal.

Some of the men went to sleep sitting up. It was difficult to sleep but I dozed off and on. Oh, how hot it was. I knew some would die down here. We had tried so hard to hang on as best as we could in the months before. Now I'm sure that some felt there would be no need to try any longer. I'm sure most of us were keenly aware that we were going to North Vietnam. I didn't seem to care any longer myself. What else could they do to us, short of killing us with their guns? We were not going home so I didn't care. I would probably never see my family again. I'm sure by now they would think we were all dead. There is no way they would know where we were being taken. Oh God, how awful to feel such painful thoughts.

The next day was much like the day before. We drank the water that was lowered down to us, and later the larger bucket was sent down to relieve ourselves. Again, the waste sloshed down over us like before and we tried to cover our heads with our hands. I began to wonder how much torture any one human being could take. I sat there in my little spot on the ship among my fellow officers in the cow poop. How many of us would make it out when we were let out of the belly of the ship?

Trying to eat the tasteless noodles was useless. Every time I tried to chew them, they ended up like a wad of glue stuck to my teeth. I would only stick to drinking the water and if I made it out alive, so be it. There was nothing left of my old self to want to motivate the others—and certainly nothing left for myself.

On about the third day out to sea, as I sat in the bottom of the filthy ship, I began thinking of my mother and father. I could see them so clearly in my mind. They were telling me to remember how I was raised. *Don't give up*, they were telling me. Think of all the education I'd had and the hard work it took to get to the level I had attained. They were telling me to shake free from the depression I was in. All at once I wanted to live! I wanted to see my family once again. I had a need to try and help my fellow officers. Oh, how I wanted to hang on a little longer!

During the fourth day out, I could feel the ship begin to move in a different direction. There were rumbling sounds coming from the old ship. Could we be docking? For the first time since we were forced down in the belly of the ship, I could hear voices. Sure enough we were docking.

Suddenly the hatch opened and light was shining through. We quickly shielded our eyes with our hands. We were told to stand up. I didn't think we could, but we did as we were told. Those who could not stand were those who had died. They had given up. It would have been so easy to give up. I almost did. We were all starving and to be put down in the belly of the old ship under those filthy conditions, I could certainly understand why those officers could see no way out but to give up.

We were told to walk out, and again we walked toward the winding stairway—only this time we were walking up. It was difficult going because we were so stiff and terribly weak. My hands trembled so much that I could hardly walk up and I had to hold on to the railing for support.

When we finally made it to the deck, we were in no condition to stand without holding on to the side of the ship. It took what seemed like forever for our eyes to adjust to the bright sunlight. It was a great feeling to breathe in the open air. It took us a while to really realize that we had made it outside. The guards passed around water for us to drink. We were given a cup of soup that was mostly water with a few grains of rice floating around inside of it. The water was passed around again and I knew better than to talk this time. We were told to walk down the plank to the ground. I was really dizzy and I noticed many of the others were swaying like me. I felt as if my body was still on the ship.

When we were assembled together, I looked around and I could see my fellow officers and I were in the worst shape we had ever been in. Our clothing was filthy with sweat and we all smelled like the belly of the ship that we had endured for four days. We were walking skeletons but we had made it to this point. A sickly bunch we were, having no idea where we would end up after surviving this horrible trip.

When we managed to walk off the ship, there were several North Vietnamese people walking around looking at us. I could tell right away that they had hate in their eyes. All at once, they began picking up rocks and throwing them at us. No one stopped them. We were the enemy out here and not only the guards disliked us, so did all of them. No one was hurt by the pelting rocks but they let us know of their distrust for us.

The guards told us to line up. Some of us could barely stand—let alone get into formation. I felt at any given moment we might keel over. Oh how weak we were! In the distance, I could see waiting buses. I wondered where we would be going this time. We were lined up to board. Oh, I prayed we would be able to do such a simple task because of our weakness. Again, we were packed inside. It was stifling hot as we bounced along to our next destination. After a while, I could see we were headed toward the jungle. What on earth would we be doing in the jungle? What were the plans of the Vietcong way out here for us to endure? Were they going to line us up and kill us all with their machine guns?

When the bus stopped, we were ordered off and I could see that we all had made it out alive but for how long I did not know. We were given a drink of water and told that we were to walk the rest of the way. I was thankful for all of the trees because they gave us some shade to make our walk a little more bearable. There were many vines growing all over the ground and some growing up into the trees. It was hard to walk without getting tangled up in the denseness and so much undergrowth. As I kept walking on, I could see bamboo growing all around us, and I couldn't get over how tall they were. Finally, we were stopped. There were guards posted in every direction. We were given another drink. We began mumbling to each other and one of the guards walked over and told us to be quiet. I'm sure all of us were wondering the same thing—what were we doing out here in the middle of nowhere?

A couple of the guards stood in front of us and we were told that we would be building our own huts out of bamboo. I didn't know about anyone else, but I had never built a hut before.

The guards began handing out knives, hatchets, and strong string. As they passed them out, we were told not to get any ideas about using them to harm the guards in any way—if we did we would be shot immediately. They let us know that at the end of the workday the tools would be taken up. They told us to remember that every tool would be accounted for. The huts that we were to build would hold 50 to 75 of us. We were divided into groups. One group would cut down the bamboo stalks. Another group would stack up the stalks, cut off the leaves and cut them to size. Another group would cut notches at each end of the stalks and secure them together with the strong string. It would take a lot of bamboo to make one hut but, as I looked around at the trees, I saw that we would have plenty to go around. At last, when the huts would be completed, we were to take the bamboo leaves and some of the stalks to make the roof to keep out the rain and other elements.

While the guards were telling us all of the details, one of them began telling us that the prisoners who were too weak to work would be the cooks for us prisoners. They pointed to several of the men and told them of their duties; they were then taken away from the rest of us. I thought, now that our own men would be cooking, we would have some decent food to eat. However, as time went on, the food was basically the same. Everything had to be cooked outside and there was no way the cooks could keep everything clean since there was no running water.

All over the jungle, each of us worked as hard as we possibly could to try to make our living quarters. We stopped only long enough to eat our little food or have a drink of water. From time to time, I would glance around and notice that we resembled a bunch of ants scurrying about. It took a while to get into a rhythm of sorts and by late afternoon we were beyond tired. When we stopped and looked at what we had completed, I was so disappointed at what we had done. We decided that in the days to come we would rotate our duties so that one person would not do more than someone else.

The guards came around to talk to us. We found out about a waterfall high up in the mountains and that there was a stream running down from the waterfall, not too far from us. This is where all of our water would be coming from—to drink and to wash our bodies. Every few days we would go there in a group of 20 to 35. We would go there in formation and the guards would be with us at all times.

That afternoon, when it was my group's turn to go there, some of us washed with our clothes on and some took theirs off. In no time, the guards shouted for us to get into formation. I didn't feel as clean as I would have liked, but getting the outer dirt washed off was a good feeling.

I had stood in the stream with my pants on and I was wet all over. I had tried to wash my shirt as well as I could. During the course of my imprisonment, I would only be given a total of four sets of clothing. As we walked out, we were astonished to find leeches all over our legs, arms, and back. When we got back, we examined each other, pulled off the blood sucking creatures, and then stomped them with our bare feet. Now we knew the stream was full of them. It was bad enough that we were starving—now we had encountered another thing to rob us of our health.

After we had eaten our meager food, we began our nightly duty to find a place to bed down. Since our huts were not completed, the ground was to become our sleeping quarters. We knew we would not sleep very well because of all the vegetation growing around. It would be next to impossible to find a place that wouldn't hurt our backs. My group decided to bed down close together so that we could keep a watch out for one another. There were ants to contend with, plus mosquitos. We were each given a piece of nylon cloth to cover ourselves.

It grew quite cold during the night—much colder than any night in South Vietnam. North Vietnam had four seasons, so we would encounter colder weather being out here. I grew very cold because I had gone into the stream with my pants on and they had not had time to dry. We would have to work harder on our huts; otherwise we would be sleeping out in the elements until then.

The next morning I felt really bad. I couldn't continue working out here without having a good night's sleep. I decided that while we were working, I would take the knife and cut away some of the growth where we would be sleeping. The trouble was, the guards were always watching what we were doing. I tried several times to slip away and cut some of the brush. I didn't get to cut away very much, but maybe what little I did would help.

I knew that some would be affected by the nights getting chilly. Sure enough, in the days ahead, I could hear coughing around the camp and no way to prevent it. The small pieces of nylon used as a cover were not going to be adequate to keep us warm enough.

Since I was able to cut away some of the undergrowth where I bedded down, I was able to sleep a little better. The mosquitos were always bothersome to all of us, and during the nights I could hear the men swatting at the little pests.

Each day, when we woke up and had our little food, we would walk out to work on our little huts. Of course we were in no condition to do such hard labor but we tried anyway.

All up and down the jungle, the poor men would be walking around stooped over, trying their best to do what they were ordered to do. They looked as if at any moment they would pass out; sometimes they would and when this happened, one of us would walk over to relieve them. Our eyes would be darting all around to make sure that the guards would not be looking.

As the days went by, we couldn't seem to be making any progress. More of the men were walking around with what I presumed to be pneumonia. It was from sleeping on the ground at night when it became so chilly. The hard coughing could be heard all over the jungle. Some coughed so hard that they would double over. I noticed one of the men spitting up blood. Oh, how many would we lose, I wondered.

To make things worse, when it would rain at night we were given a piece of plastic to cover our bodies. It didn't do any good because we would eventually be lying in water.

I don't know the total number of prisoners we had out there, some were already there when my group arrived. I guessed there were several hundred. We were all working building our huts. There was very little talking. We were so used to not talking that the few times we whispered to one another, it seemed out of place. The guards were always ready to shout at us if anyone tried.

One morning while we were eating, the guards began shouting to each other. I looked up in time to see several of them carrying out some of the prisoners. I could tell they had died during the night. I don't know where they carried them. The poor souls' little limbs looked like matchsticks. We all turned away and glanced at each other and shook our heads. It was another sad time for us. I don't think I would ever get used to seeing death.

One day, as my group was walking out to the stream to wash our filthy bodies, we saw in the distance what looked like a family. As we passed them one of the guards shouted, "Don't talk to these men. They are crazy. They might want to kill you." They were talking about us. The family kept walking on back, I guess, to where they lived. Every once in a while they would turn their heads toward us.

I didn't know anyone lived out here. I suppose they had a little farm nearby. We later learned that they were the Highland Tribe that lived high in the mountains.

As the days went by, we made a little more progress building our huts. If we were healthy we could finish much quicker. It was hard labor and we were so weak. Just dragging the bamboo around took most of our energy. We had scrapes and cuts all over our arms and legs. Sometimes, while I was walking back and forth, my heart would begin to pound in my chest and it was hard to catch my breath. The only time we could rest was when we would stop to have a drink— which was not very often. There were times when I could easily have dropped to the ground and never gotten up, but the guards were always watching us.

My gums had begun to bother me again. They would swell and hurt so terribly. One night, as I was preparing to bed down, one of my back teeth fell out onto the ground. Maybe it wouldn't hurt so much now, I thought. I started thinking about my teeth. I didn't like it one bit that I had lost another tooth. It should never have happened. I have always taken such good care of my health. This was so senseless.

When we first arrived in the jungle, and the guards had handed out the tools to help build the huts, I noticed right away that none on the tools were as sharp as they should have been. Over a period of time, with so many of us using them, they had become very dull.

One morning, as I was hacking away trying to cut away the stalk from one of the trees, I had my hand holding the stalk and in my other hand I held the hatchet. All at once, the hatchet slipped and I cut my arm at the elbow all the way down to my wrist. Blood spurted and dripped all over me. I suddenly felt like throwing up. One of my buddies came running over and tried to help me. I took off my filthy shirt and wrapped it around my arm very tightly. I knew the cut needed to be washed, otherwise it might get infected.

There was no clean water anywhere and no medication to put on the wound. I had to hope it would stop bleeding, and it finally did. Later that afternoon when my group went to the stream, I walked as far upstream as I could, trying to find cleaner water, and there I washed my arm as best as I could. One of my buddies washed the shirt to try to get the blood out. When I finished washing, I put the shirt back on. I hoped that the cut would soon heal but I had my doubts.

The following days after my accident, there was not much I could do to help the men finish building the hut. I tried to do little things such as ripping the leaves off the bamboo but my wound opened up and began to bleed. I wanted to keep it as clean as possible. My buddies did all they could to fill in for me.

Now that I had time to think of things other than working, I began to take stock of the men in my group, and myself. Our uniforms were rags now and we had not had a change of clothing in months. Some of the prisoners had ripped off the bottom half of their pants. So much of the material was barely hanging together, plus mud was caked all over them and it was much easier to walk without carrying around the extra weight. So many of the men suffered from diarrhea; others including myself, suffered from what I assumed was arthritis. Our knees were swollen, making it difficult to walk correctly. Some of the men had died of pneumonia, and others walked around with hard coughs. Nosebleeds, sore throats, and earaches were always bothersome. One of the things that bothered us was the soles of our feet. They were so packed with dirt that we never seemed to be able to wash it off. Our toenails were long and black. None of us wore shoes—any shoes we had on when we were captured had rotted and fallen apart long ago. My feet ached all the time. We all had cuts and scrapes and it's a wonder that we were able to stand and walk at all.

One night, a horrible thing happened to the group of officers that bedded down next to us. One of the officers, who was already very ill, began biting around the inside of his wrist until it began to bleed. He wouldn't let anyone help him. He had reached a point where he couldn't go any longer. He kept biting chunks of flesh and he bled to death during the night. The next morning, he was dragged out by the guards to wherever they carried the dead. This was another low point for all of us. It was especially hard on me since I was unable to work because of my arm, and not having anything to do except think made everything else that much more difficult.

None of us heard from our families. I think if we could have let them know where we were, we would be able to rest a little better. I tried not to go there very often in my thoughts.

I began thinking about the food we ate out here. The officers who did our cooking had no way to keep our food clean. They had a difficult time going back and forth to the stream to get the water that they used. The water they used was the same water we bathed in and drank from. All of it came from the same place. As the weeks went by, most of us became sick with dysentery. If we didn't eat, we would surely die and if we continued to get our water from the stream, we would become sicker. It all came down to this: we didn't have a choice in the matter.

The day finally came—we had completed our hut. It wasn't the best construction, but to us it was a castle. We now had a place to sleep, and this was all that mattered.

By now my arm was almost healed. That cut left a long, rough scar, but I was thankful that it caused no threat of an infection. I knew I had to be more careful with the tools. Once in a while, other officers would cut themselves, but I saw no one cut themselves as badly as I had.

One day as I was helping another group complete their hut, one of the officers motioned to me to look at something he was pointing to. There, under one of the bushes, was a small bundle. At first neither one of us wanted to touch it. With much hesitation I reached for it and opened it. Inside were sweet potatoes and a type of sweetener made from rice. We stared at it for a while and then decided it was most likely from the family we saw when walking to the stream to wash our bodies.

They had not taken the guards' warning about us being crazy. The little gift was their way of showing their concern for us and wanting to help keep us from starving to death. These little bundles were found every so often. We shared them with those around us. The guards never noticed us finding them, which we were thankful about.

Over a period of time out in the jungle, my dreams changed. Every time I went to sleep, I now woke up having dreams about my wife and family. I would see my wife so clearly and no matter how much I tried to catch hold of her arm, she would pull away. The dream was always in slow motion. Sometimes my parents would be in the dream, but it always ended up with my wife screaming with blood all around her.

They always left me with a feeling of hopelessness. I always thought if I could just hear from my family, I would stop having these dreams. How wrong I was again.

Almost everyone was able to finish their huts. Some of the huts were built better than others, but I knew we were happy to be out of the elements.

One morning the guards came around and told us to stand at attention. They told us that we would be making gardens. We looked at each other, and I'm sure we all thought the same thing. Now, at last, we would finally have something decent to eat! We were given tools to dig up weeds and the many vines growing everywhere. After clearing the land, we dug up the dirt and turned it over. Finally, we planted beans, corn, and rice. All over the jungle, different groups were preparing the ground for the gardens.

Oh, how hot and humid it was. The work was back breaking. We had now entered the hot and rainy season, and most everyone was starved so badly we had no energy to do such hard work. Once in a while one of the men would start swaying and one of us, with the side of our hip, would prop him up long enough so he could gain control again. Sometimes it would be me helping them, and other times it would be them helping me. This happened so many times during our imprisonment and it became commonplace.

It seemed to take forever to clear the land. Each day, my group of about sixty men would walk out and begin to try to work. It wouldn't be long until one of us would have to stop and rest for a moment because of being so weak. We had to be very careful because of the guards. Finally, we completed the clearing.

Early one morning as we were turning the soil, one of the officers who was beside me leaned over and pulled out a long earthworm. He promptly put it into his mouth. "Good nutrition!" he whispered. He motioned for me to try one. I pulled one out and tried to eat it. All at once my stomach felt as if I would throw up. When he saw that I wasn't going to eat it, he took the wiggly thing and popped it into his mouth. Oh God, it had come to this: eating worms to stay alive so that we could continue to work like dogs.

CHAPTER FOUR

PRISON YEARS

W e would work all day out in the garden and finally the day came that we could start seeding. We squatted almost all day long and when we tried to stand, it was almost impossible. My knees hurt almost as much as my back. When I tried to lie down at night I was in so much pain. I knew my knees needed to be drained because of the fluid around them. There was nothing I could do but bear the pain. I started thinking about the last time that I could walk, stand, and lie down easily, but I couldn't remember. All of my fellow officers, I'm sure, were in pain. It didn't make matters any better but I couldn't complain because we were all in this together.

One day, a couple of the guards walked by while we were working. They began telling us to dump our waste from the hole onto the garden for fertilizer. Every time there was a lull in our work day, we were told to do something else. They did not want us to take a break. There was never a time for us to take care of ourselves.

We took buckets and filled them with the waste and dumped the stinking mess on the garden. Others would spread the waste all around the garden. It seemed like forever before we completed the task. The stench was awful and the reason for taking so long was our latrine was a long way from the garden.

I think there comes a time when the body is so depleted that you can't react to how you feel. This was where most of us were at the time. We had a job to do and no matter how disgusting or how badly we felt, we did it.

It was becoming more difficult to sleep. I was in so much pain that rest would not come for me. I constantly kept thinking how good it would feel to be able to sit down in a tub of hot water and just stay there for a couple of hours to let each muscle relax. Of course it was only a thought—a thought that would never become a reality.

We were in this particular part of the jungle for about five months when the guards told us one morning that our group would be moving. I no longer thought about going home. The guards knew we all wanted to go home more than anything else in the world. It seemed they only wanted us to keep moving. Early the next morning, we were told to line up in formation. We did as we were told. I could see that not all of the prisoners were leaving—only my group of about 55 men. I supposed the other prisoners would follow later on.

We were leaving before the garden was ready. I had thought we would probably not be able to eat any of the vegetables anyway. I knew from the beginning something would happen but I never thought we would be leaving. It was always difficult to think ahead of the Vietcong. Just when we thought we knew something, they would fool us and plans would turn completely opposite from what we thought.

It was hot as we walked to our new destination. We stopped only once for a drink of water. We didn't stop to rest until finally we were told to stop. There was nothing there except more of the same jungle that we had left. It meant we would have to build our huts again. Could we start completely from scratch once again? It would have been good to be able to sit down while the guards told us what we were to do; instead we were told to stand at attention as they told us. We would be divided into teams. Yes, we would be building our huts again out here. We gathered from what the guards were saying that the other prisoners would be joining us and they would be clearing the land for a garden while we built the huts. None of us had any say-so in the decisions that were made, so we would do as we were told.

As the guards were talking to us, we could hear other prisoners marching toward us. As they drew closer, we saw the pitiful officers trying to stay in formation. They held their heads high. They, like us, were in rags. Some of them were wearing only part of the old uniform. They looked as if they might fall down. It almost made me cry and it was difficult to look at them because we were looking at ourselves at the same time. Even though this happened so many times, it was always a shock to see the similarity.

The guards passed around the rusty and dull knives, saws, and string to us. We were once again divided into groups. We already knew what to do, but the guards kept telling us how to use each thing. I had already decided to be very careful and not hurt myself like I had before.

We walked out and began the cutting and stacking. It was hot and tiring but we kept on working. We stopped only to have a drink. At the end of the work day we finally had another drink. We were told that we would not be going to the stream to wash our bodies. It was too late to walk there and get back before dark. The same cooks that we had before had prepared our little meal. It was exactly like the other meals that they had prepared.

We ate, and afterwards we stumbled around trying to find a place to bed down for the night. We were all beyond tired. We were once again given the small piece of nylon to cover ourselves. I slept better than I thought I would. I hoped the other officers did as well.

Each day was much like the day before. Eat our little meal, work, and fall exhausted on the ground to sleep. There was no time to feel sorry for ourselves. We had a job to do and we did it. Most of the time we acted in the manner that we were trained—hold our heads high and do as we were told. One night, one of the men decided to make a break for it and leave. The officers near him whispered to him to think twice about it. No amount of trying to reason with him did any good. Like the other prisoner at the second place we were held, this prisoner left in the middle of the night. We couldn't imagine him wanting to leave. We were in North Vietnam. It would be impossible to get out. He left anyway.

The next morning I eased myself up still thinking about the prisoner. I looked all around, but I didn't see him anywhere. Could he have made it out, I thought.

While we were eating our breakfast, we heard loud talking and shouting. In the distance we could see guards pulling the prisoner in front of us. One of the guards was carrying a rope. Right in the middle of us, the guards pushed the prisoner to one of the trees and the guard with the rope tied him tightly with it. One of the guards shouted to all of us, "Let this be an example to you. Run away and you will be caught!"

All over the jungle, it was so quiet. I kept thinking I couldn't see this happening again. How terrible. The prisoner became like a crazy person. He was crying and screaming at the same time. We were told, just as before, to give the prisoner no eye contact, no water, and say nothing to him.

It was another low point for all of us officers. It hurt so badly. We could do nothing. We were told to go about our work. We did as we were told. There was no way to drown out the screaming.

It was a very long day. There are no words to express the anger and helplessness I felt. I could only pray it would end very soon.

The prisoner died during the night. After we had bedded down for the night, he suddenly stopped screaming—I knew then that he was out of his misery. Months ago, when the first prisoner decided to leave and was tied to a tree to die, I thought I would not be able to go through this again. I did go through it and so did all of my fellow officers. It wasn't that we were so strong and could handle anything. No, it was because this was the way we lived out here. We were prisoners and because we had no recourse, we swallowed our feelings, choked back our tears, and went on doing what we were told to do.

I thought about my family. The children were growing up without their father. I was of no help to my Lien. I missed her so much. I thought about my parents. I knew they worried about me. I'm sure they thought I was dead. Somehow this gave me comfort. If I were dead they wouldn't have to worry about how I was being treated or about my health. But I was not dead. I was trying so hard to stay alive. It would be so easy to let myself go crazy. I had seen enough of how easy it was first to give up and let my mind go insane. I had to think positively. I kept wrestling with my emotions. So many have died. Some because of starving and some because they could see no way out. I began telling myself and questioning myself. What do I have to hang on to?

I finally decided that I had lived this long, so I would continue to live. I would survive this horror. I had to be strong for my family and I knew that one day I would be with them again.

As the days passed, we finished one hut, then another. How we were able to get this done, I didn't know. We just did.

Our trips to the stream were not as often as before. I guess because it was farther away. The times that I did get to go meant not only would feel better and cleaner but walking there meant getting away from so much sameness. I was very weak and my knees hurt terribly—but no matter how much I hurt physically, I knew emotionally it was comforting. I always looked forward to the walk there and back.

The prisoners I was around for so long became very close. We never talked, only mouthed to each other once in a while, but we were as close as brothers. We helped each other out so many times with nothing more than a shake of our head or a motion with our eyes. I knew that when we finally got the chance to go back home, these fellow officers would be my closest friends for the rest of my life. One day, we were told to start a garden. All over the jungle some were still building huts and others, like my group, were given the same rusty tools to begin working on clearing the land to make the garden.

We worked every day out in the hot humid heat clearing the ground. Finally the day came when we turned the soil to begin the planting. All up and down the garden, the officers could be seen pulling out the fat earthworms and eating them as if they were a delicacy one would eat in a fancy restaurant.

One day I finally decided that I should eat one of the worms. Why not? Everyone else was. I pulled the fat wiggly worm out and popped him in my mouth. I began to feel it moving around and I tried to swallow it but in the process I threw up. I tried it again, but gave up. I wondered if any of the others had the same experience as me.

I don't know how we were able to go through the motions of preparing the land for the garden. We did as we were forced to do. My knees hurt me so much that in comparison to my other medical problems, they took predominance over everything. They were so swollen with fluid that I could barely move about. There was nothing I could do but keep going. At night, I would sit up and rub them. It really didn't help very much but that's all I could think to do.

Another officer died during the time we were working in the garden. He just fell over and we all thought he would come around with the other officers nearby helping him, but it was no use. I imagined his heart just gave out.

All of us were saddened because of his death. It was a pitiful time for us when the guards pulled him out to drag his body to wherever the others who had died were put.

Death never came easily for us; although we felt like crying, we went back to whatever we were doing before he died. This is what we did. What else could we do?

We had our visitors again. The communists came to talk to us about changing our way of thinking and becoming one of them. Like so many of the others officers did, I tuned them out. I thought about my family or about what I wished I could have to eat. Like the other times, we sat up straight and looked right at them. Did they actually think we would change our minds? The funny thing was when I would think about it. I would look directly at them and think about anything except what they were saying. I had gotten quite good at this. That was one test I would fail, that is, if we were tested on what was said.

Some of the plants were beginning to come up and it would be so wonderful to finally eat the produce. As we were hoeing around the plants one day, the guards told us we must throw our waste on the plants for fertilizer. I was hoping that they would forget about doing this, but they had not. We began the backbreaking task of loading the filthy waste into buckets and carrying it out to the garden. The smell was unbearable. It took many trips to finally complete the task.

Three or four weeks later, we began the task of picking some of the vegetables. The garden still smelled of the stench of waste. It was not easy to pick the vegetables and even worse to dig the potatoes because of having to dig around the soil. Before long, we had picked several baskets of onions, beans, and potatoes. The corn was looking good but we needed to leave it awhile because it was not ready to be harvested. We had also planted rice—but the other prisoners took care of this area.

As we picked the vegetables, the guards carried the baskets to some other location. We were so excited about getting to taste some of our hard labor. When the evening meal was served, I was so disappointed that we had our usual food. Maybe next time we would have some of the vegetables.

As the days passed, only once did we have anything from the garden. Our cooks put some of the beans with our rice. They were not cooked very well and had no taste, but it was something different. I suppose the vegetables went to the guards and their families; we never saw them again.

Once in a while, as we were picking the vegetables, we would put a vegetable in our mouths and quickly eat it. After a while some of us would get very sick. I don't know if it was from eating so fast or if it was the fertilizer that we put on the crops that made us so ill. It could have been a combination of both. The whole deal with the garden made us really angry. All of the hard work for nothing. I wondered if the garden was meant for the prisoners but like everything else, we were left out.

When the corn was ready to be harvested, it smelled so sweet as we pulled it off of the stalks. This is the one crop that I wanted more than most. I decided one way or another I was going to have some of the corn. When the guards were talking to each other, I quickly pulled away the husk and began eating the sweet raw corn. I was able to eat about half when all at once I became very sick. My stomach swelled up and the pain made me double over. Oh, how awful I felt. Not only was I sick, but I lost another tooth again.

When our working day finally ended, it was all I could do to make it back to the hut. I did not eat the evening meal; in fact I was sick most of the night. At last morning finally came and I felt better and never again did I try to eat any of the corn from the garden.

We had been at this particular place for about five months when we found out, one morning, that we would be moving once again. I didn't know why we had to move so often. Maybe it was for security reasons. Nothing surprised me anymore. If we were moving then we were moving. The worst thing about leaving was the fact that we would have to build our huts again. I would not be thrilled about this.

My group was down to about 48 now, and when we gathered together early one morning we were told to line up in formation. We did as we were told. We marched out without being told how far we would march. To our surprise we only walked about two-and-a-half miles. When we stopped to have a drink, I couldn't believe my eyes!

There were huts all around! We wouldn't have to build them this time. I began thinking, maybe this was not where we would be living. I thought we would start marching again, but to my surprise and the others' amazement, this was actually where we would be staying. No one said a word. What did we do to deserve such luck?

The guards kept us in formation and told us that we would be busy out here making another garden. We could do this. What other choice did we have?

Another surprise for us was that we were a little closer to the stream than the location that we'd just left.

At last, we were told to leave formation and that we could go to the stream to bathe. We were so hot and sweaty—to be able to wash ourselves was a treat.

We again lined up and headed for the stream. Our uniforms were all but rotted away. We all had a piece of a shirt here and rags for the bottoms there. We quickly washed ourselves as best we could and walked back to the huts to begin the task of pulling off the leeches and stomping them with our bare feet. It seems impossible to be conditioned to the way of life out here—having nothing much to eat, the hard work we did every day, drinking and bathing in the same water, no medical supplies, and seeing so much sadness. How we did this all in stride is beyond my thinking. It was just the way we lived.

Sometimes it was almost like we were not civilized anymore. Sometimes I would wonder what our families would think if they saw us out here. I didn't think about it very often, but sometimes I wondered if we were human at all.

As each day passed, we lost more prisoners to starvation. Some of them were friends of mine and although the others were not, their deaths made me sad because we were all officers out here trying to hold on a little longer.

At night, my dreams would come as soon as I dropped off to sleep. One night I must have been screaming because one of the officers near me shook me awake. Oh, God, how awful the dreams were. Again, my wife was in them and, like always, all I could see was blood everywhere. When I would try to reach for her, all of this was done in slow motion.

One night, I decided to try to think of happy thoughts about my children or something funny that happened while I was in training. Thinking of such thoughts, I assumed, would cause me not to dream about death and such horrible things. It did not help. No matter what I would be thinking, I still continued to have them. I knew all of the other officers had them because I could hear them moaning in the night. We had to be very careful about making any kind of commotion in the night for fear the guards would come and pull us out and take us away.

Out in the jungle, in North Vietnam, we had four seasons. We never saw snow, but in the nighttime it could get very cold. There were many times that all of us felt like we were going to freeze to death. I'm positive that some of the officers who died during the cold months died because of the weather and all of the ailments we all encountered.

One night as I lay in the hut, I began to figure out how long we had been here. To the best of my ability, I guessed five years—because of the number of seasons I remembered. When I was first captured, I kept thinking we would be released at any given moment. Now as I lay thinking about the time, all I could think about was what a waste of valuable time. My children growing up without me, my wife having to rear the children alone, my parents grieving for me—it was almost too much to think about. I again had to think of something positive. Anything to get my mind from thinking crazy thoughts. I hated thinking these thoughts because they didn't help in any way to make the situation any better. I finally went to sleep only to wake up having had my usual dream.

We moved five more times out in the jungle. Sometimes we would have to build our own huts and other times we would march out and find them already built. This always made us feel good to not have to build again. Since all the prisoners were moved so many times, we used each other's huts on so many occasions. One day, we had a lull in our always busy schedule. It didn't happen very often and on this particular day, two guards walked by and, seeing us resting, told us to stand at attention. We could tell they were angry at us. We were told to go and clean out a ditch nearby. It was full of dead leaves and stagnant water. Now there was no need to clean out the ditch as it served no purpose. Cleaning out this area was their way of telling us that since we had nothing better to do, they would find us something.

We lined up in formation and—taking shovels and hoes with us—marched out to the ditch. As we approached, we began walking around and disturbed thousands of mosquitoes. They began biting us all over. Some of the men had taken off their shirts before they left because they knew it would be a hot job and they wanted to be comfortable.

This was not the best of ideas. I could see large welts coming up on the men. Some of the men tried to run from the mosquitoes but no matter where they ran, they would be followed by the pests. We worked very fast and finally finished the job of cleaning. When we began to march back, I noticed the welts on the men had turned into large bumps. The men soon became disoriented and I could see that they were very sick.

When we got back to our huts, those of us who were not sick tried to attend to the sick men. I ran to where the cooks were cooking our evening meal and I used my shirt to dip into a bucket of water. I ran back to the men and tried to cool them down. It was no use. These men were terribly sick. Their skin had turned yellow. At once, I knew that they had malaria. For those of us who were not sick, I knew we had all been inoculated for many diseases, including the one for malaria. We received these shots before we travelled to the US.

In a matter of a few days, we lost 15 of our best men. How I hated the Vietcong. This was a senseless death for all of the men who died. We felt terrible, especially since they had lasted all of this time to end up dying in this manner. We would never get used to death. I wished it could have been our captors instead.

As the weeks and months passed by, I tried my best to figure out how long we had been in the jungle of North Vietnam. I concluded we had been here for over six years.

One day, we were told that we would be able to write to our families. Why now after all of this time, I wondered. There was no way we could understand the Vietcong and the decisions they made. It would be a relief to finally put our thoughts down on paper and let our loved ones know where we were. We were given a small notepad, a pen, and an envelope. We were told that our families would have to send us more supplies when we needed them. We were also told we could receive packages as well.

At the end of our work day, and after we had eaten our little food, all over the jungle I knew everyone would be in a hurry to do their letter writing. So many months ago, I thought about all the things I would say to my family if we could only write to them. Now, as I sat with my notepad in my hand, I couldn't think of anything to say, especially something encouraging. We had seen so much sickness and death. I finally said something about us getting to write and to let them know that I was in good health—this wasn't exactly true but I couldn't tell them how I really was. I didn't want to worry them unnecessarily. We completed our letters and they were collected—we knew we wouldn't get a reply for a while. When we finally did, they were over a month old. This was because we could only write once a month and receive them at the same time.

After several months, we began to receive many letters at once—because they had been held back. Of course, the letters would all have been opened.

Soon we had a big bundle of letters that each one of us protected with our lives. They became more precious than gold. They were read and reread many times. They gave us something to look forward to and a reason to hang on a little longer.

One day, I received a large package as well as a letter from my wife. Everyone was well at home. There was always news about the children. I always liked to hear all the things they were doing.

After our evening meal, the guards brought out the packages that had been delivered. Inside mine were several pairs of socks. I couldn't wear socks because I didn't have any shoes. After thinking about it, I decided that I could wear them at night when it would get cold. There were some toiletries as well. As always there was some packaged food. I divided it with those near me. Some of the packages of the food had been opened and the guards had eaten some of it. This always angered me, but there was nothing I could do about it. One evening, as we were all reading our mail, one of the men began reading his and with trembling hands he began to softly cry. When he regained his composure, he whispered that his wife had met someone else and was leaving him. She believed he was never getting out of prison. I felt sorry for him. I knew that if we didn't keep an eye out for him, he might give up and we didn't need to lose another one.

I began to think of my own wife. Did she ever have these thoughts? I thought about this many times in the coming weeks.

Another good thing was happening. We could now have visitors. The trouble was, it was so far away from our homes. Only once in a while would someone travel all these many miles to come to visit their son or husband.

We were out working one morning when one of the guards came up to me and told me I had a visitor. I turned around and saw my beautiful Lien standing beside the table where visitors could talk to their family. Her father's brother had come with her to protect her and to carry her belongings. The guard told Lien to sit at one end of the table and me at the other one. The guard sat between us. I was totally shocked that she had come such a long distance to see me. She told me they had taken a train and two buses, and had walked the many miles through the jungle of North Vietnam. She told me her father had paid all of their travel expenses. Lien looked so very tired.

We talked for a few minutes and without thinking, I told her she should find someone else because I didn't think I was ever getting out. She let out a mournful cry. I didn't know what else to say. I was stunned at what I had said. The guard told us that our time was up and that she should go. Lien pushed a large sack to the guard that she had taken from her uncle. She got up, still looking shocked, and then she and her uncle left to go back the way they had come.

What had I done to my beautiful Lien? Why did I say such hurtful things to her? Part of me knew I was right to tell her, and part of me wanted to just lie down and cry. My poor sweet Lien had looked so tired. I knew I had hurt her deeply. I kept seeing her face with the look of unbelief on it. How would I ever be able to live with myself again?

The rest of the day I vaguely remember. I must have gone through the motions of whatever we always did. That evening, I was given the sack. There were many precious things inside for me. Medication and more packaged food.

The weeks went by, with all of my fellow officers and me trying to hang on. At last, a month had passed and we received our mail. I quickly went to our hut and opened several letters from home. Some were from my parents and I put them aside to read later. I was shaking as I opened Lien's letter. It sounded so hopeful and she never mentioned anything about the hurtful things I had told her when she visited me. I felt tears on my cheeks as I read her sweet letter. As time went on, we never mentioned the hurtful things I had said. I knew she had been terribly hurt but all was forgiven and at last I was at peace with myself.

The seasons came and went out in the jungle. We continued to work every day, whether it was in the garden or building huts. The letters still came from home and I don't think many of the officers would have made it without hearing from their families. These letters helped to keep us sane.

Lien came to see me once more. Oh, what joy just to see her sweet face! She brought pictures of the children. I probably would not have known who they were had she not told me. They were growing up so fast. I couldn't hold back my tears looking at their little faces. We chatted a little longer. She had come with her uncle again to help protect her and to carry her belongings. They had taken a train and two buses, and the two of them had walked the many miles through the jungle just to see me for 10 minutes. Oh, how strong my Lien was. I shuddered to think she could have been taken ill or even been killed—she was taking such a risk coming to see me. I learned how brave she really was! In my mind she was much braver than me.

We lost two more of the officers through sickness or starvation. It was never easy to see them one day and the next day they would be gone.

My knees, and the knees of some of the other officers, were still painful to move about. All of us received medication from our families but most of us needed to be under the care of a doctor. We never received any kind of proper care.

In May 1982, the officers and I moved once more. We were told one morning that we were leaving. We presumed it was to another part of the jungle so we went about not being anxious about where it would be. After all, we had moved so many times before. We walked for several hours, stopping only to have a drink of water. By now the officers and I were baffled as to where we were going. I don't know how many miles we walked; I only knew it was many.

We came to a clearing and we saw that we were out of the jungle. By my estimation, we had been in the jungle for seven years. At last we came to a clearing and we were crossing over railroad tracks. We kept on marching until we came to a passenger car. Could we be so lucky to actually be going in this passenger car and not in the old smelly cattle car? We were being treated as human beings! This was almost unbelievable!

Before long, the guards walked around with chains. We were chained two by two instead of being all chained together. They went all up and down the line chaining us with a fellow prisoner. We finally entered the train and sat down in regular seats. I didn't mind being chained because we had one hand free. As we sat there waiting until we would be moving, I whispered to my fellow officer next to me. "Could we possibly be going back to South Vietnam?"

"Yes," he whispered to me, "it surely looks that way."

It was very hot traveling, but we kept all of the windows lowered so that we could be as cool as possible.

We stayed on the train for three days—three long days sitting up. We dozed off and on during that time. At each place that the train stopped we were able to stand up while we drank warm water. We were given dried food to eat, which wasn't much but it kept us alive to keep moving on.

At the end of three traveling days on the train, we finally stopped. The guards shouted for us to stay seated. We were back in South Vietnam. We were so tired but thankful we would be closer to our families.

As I sat next to my fellow officer, I saw a small piece of paper on the floor. I leaned over hurriedly and picked it up. I reached into my pocket for my pen and while the guards were not looking, I wrote that I was back in the South. On the back I wrote my parents' address. There were several Vietnamese standing near the train and I threw the paper out of the window. I had no idea if one of them would pick it up or even take the note to my family. There would be no way that any of our loved ones would know we were back. I only hoped some brave person would deliver it for me. The guard shouted to us to stand at attention, and in an orderly fashion we got off the train. We were happy to be back in the South. We all tried not to show our excitement with our faces but inside we were overjoyed to be so close to them.

We had left the jungle after being there for seven years.

We stood at attention after we got off of the train. It was very hot and humid and I knew right away we were entering into the rainy season.

We were back in South Vietnam but we were still prisoners. We began to march in formation. Since we were never told where we were marching to, we did as we were told. We stopped only once to have a drink of water, and then we continued on. Finally we entered into a camp that we later learned was Z-30C Ham Tan in Saigon. We were at last unchained. It was good to have both hands free but my wrist was raw from the constant rubbing.

We had a chance to look around. We were in a large compound which would house 60 to 75 prisoners. There were two floors, which would hold the same amount of prisoners. There were other buildings with two floors so they would hold many others.

In the following days, the excitement of being back gradually wore off. We found out that nothing had really changed for us. We continued to have very little to eat. The guards still shouted at us and the living conditions were deplorable. On our third day at the camp, one of the men died after being very sick. We had no medication to give him and he died in his sleep.

We were divided up into groups. We were ordered once again to make gardens. At this time I believe all of the remaining prisoners from the jungle had arrived and we were housed in and around the compound together.

I was once again downcast about my note I had written to my family. I was positive that the note had not been delivered to them. I could visualize the note was still on the ground and had most likely been blown away by a gust of wind. No, nothing had changed. I was closer to my family out here, and I was truly thankful for this, but even if my family came to visit, I could still no longer touch them. I so wanted to be home with my Lien and our children.

In my mind, I began to scream. It was a mournful scream that no one could hear. They were tucked deep into my mind. I had to let my frustration out. Big tears fell down my face. I was all alone with my thoughts. How could I be so close to my family but still be so far away from them?

That evening it began to rain. At bedtime, I walked into our area of the room to bunk down. It was another low point for me.

We were at the compound for four days when we began to have families come to visit us. One of the officers whispered to me, after he'd had a visitor, that someone carried the note to my family. Oh, how thankful I was that someone was brave enough to deliver it!

That morning, as I was cutting down the tall weeds, a guard came up to me to tell me that I had a visitor.

I walked up to where Lien was standing and I could see the relief in her eyes as she smiled at me. I hugged her in my heart.

We once again sat at a long table with the guard in the middle and Lien and me at opposite ends. As usual it was difficult to talk in the way we would have liked with the guard sitting right there.

I told her it was good to see her and I know she felt the same way. We chatted for a while and she told me that my parents would be coming to see me very soon. Our 10 minutes were up way too soon. The guard told me to return to my duties. She left telling me she would come again. Oh, how I hated to see her leave.

One thing that made my life somewhat easier, especially emotionally, was one of my fellow officers—who had already been in prison a while before I was captured. I had been aware of him but I never got to interact with him in any way. He was a Baptist minister from South Vietnam and he too was Vietnamese. He was also a Major. I happened to see him one day and as usual he seemed to always have his head bowed as if he was thinking about something very deep. He saw me staring at him as he looked up. I guess he could tell that I was wondering what he was thinking about. He whispered to me, "I am praying for all of the prisoners out here. I am a pastor and I am a chaplain for all of you." Even though I was not his religion, he always gave me comfort and made me think a little more positively. He made me feel safe whenever I saw him after this encounter. Over a period of the months to come I learned that he was treated more severely than any of us ever thought. If anyone were religious in any way, they were captured and their life was hell from then on. I learned he was older than most of us. He always seemed to be smiling and I often wondered how he could be so calm and at peace. Another thing I found out was the higher in rank we were, the longer we stayed in prison. Over a period of time, I was also to learn whenever a prisoner left us, especially if they were a lower rank, we assumed they had died, but actually not all of them died. They were let go after they had served their time.

During the first years of our imprisonment, we would get all excited about making a garden. Now, it was no longer exciting and happy thoughts we felt, but a chore that we had to do for the Vietcong. We were never to get the pleasure of eating the fruits of our labor.

Working in the garden was one more thing we had to do. The guards never failed to mention to us to throw our waste on the garden for fertilizer. It was still a filthy job and very tiring, but somehow we always managed to do this backbreaking task.

In the compound where we were staying, I estimated there to be 700 men. As usual, we were to never talk to each other. At the beginning I missed talking and so did all of the prisoners. After a few years without communication, it became easier to just think in our minds. For the most part, my mind stayed fairly good. The only time we could talk was if we had a visitor. I mostly let my folks do the talking. We never had any news to tell anyway and talking seemed so strange. I found it easier to just listen.

Nothing ever changed for us. We went about our daily work all morning, stopped for a drink, and then back to work. We stopped for our midday meal of rice and manias and then back to work again. Then we would have a small meal and fall into our bunks, exhausted.

My mother and father came to see me one afternoon. As usual it was good to see them. My mother never failed to tell me how bad I looked. She would never know how badly we were treated—maybe they both knew this already but I would never mention it to either one.

The next time I saw my wife, she brought the children with her. Hieu was at this time around 12. The girls were dressed so beautifully. I was so proud of them. My wife did a lot of sewing to make extra money and she also saw that the children had nice clothing. My in-laws were so kind to them and helped my wife in so many ways all the years that I was in prison.

On one of my wife's visits, she told me that when Hieu turned nine years old, she made him a beautiful birthday cake and he insisted that they sell the cake to help the family out financially. This brought tears to my eyes to think that such a young boy was to think beyond his years. I would never forget this.

Every time my family came to visit they always brought packages of food, which they had to hand to the guards and, like always, when I received them, they would have opened them and taken out what they wanted. There was not only food but toiletries and medication. I was always happy to get anything they brought with them.

Each day that it wasn't raining, we would be out in the garden. During the rainy season there were always lots of weeds. We planted the usual—beans, corn, onions, and rice.

Each night, many of us would wake up after having our dreadful dreams. Mine never changed. Night after night, year after year, I would be shaken awake by a buddy because I'd been moaning or crying. The dreams were still of me trying to catch my wife with blood everywhere. Going to sleep each night was never a peaceful thing for me to do. I dreaded it every night. Some nights I never slept at all—thank goodness this did not happen often. There would be no way I could work as hard as we had to without sleep.

Out here, in the back of each barracks, we had running water. We no longer had to travel to get our bath in a stream. I really missed walking out to do this. The water out back was cold or sometimes lukewarm depending on the weather. We would wash ourselves as best as we could with our hands. Some of us had towels and washcloths and a bar of soap that were sent to us from our families. They did help—that is, until they got dirty.

We still had officers dying. It hurt terribly when we lost them. We had become so close to each other and to lose one was almost unbearable. It was never easy.

My group of about 40 men had been in Z-30C for about three months when we were told that we would be moving. We finished our little meal and got into formation. Once again, we were marching to another place. The Vietcong wanted us to always be moving. I no longer cared. We continued to march for about one-and-a-half hours, stopped for a drink, and then we continued on. Finally we reached another compound. We were told to begin making a latrine. We were given shovels and a group began to dig. I wondered how many of these things we had dug—too many to count, I thought.

The compound was basically the same as the one we had just left. They were dirty and smelled from the officers who had left to be moved someplace else.

By now, the rainy season was over and the hot weather was upon us. We were completely soaked with sweat from digging the latrine. Of course it came as no surprise that we would be planting a garden again. The guards began telling us how to clean the land for the garden. We always had to stand in formation while they went on and on about it. Why they did this to us would always be a mystery. Once again, the weakest prisoners would be the cooks.

We had our little noon meal and the guards brought out the tools—that by now were past dullness.

After our little meal, we walked out to the area where we were to be making the garden. To our surprise, the garden was all ready to be seeded. The prisoners before us had done the backbreaking task of getting the area cleaned and the soil turned; then they were told to move out. I felt sorry for the men but we were happy to continue what they had done.

While we were planting the seeds, my heart started to beat very fast as it had done years ago when we were first captured. It was difficult to breathe. I took several deep breaths and tried to calm my heart. It acted up several times that day and was bothersome to me. I certainly didn't want to be the next officer to die out here.

Before the day ended for us out in the garden, one of the men whispered to me that he hurt very badly in his lower back. He told me he thought it was his kidneys. I put my hand over his forehead and sure enough he had a high fever. We went back to planting the seeds. Soon afterward, the man fell over. I quickly walked over to him and tried to walk him back to the barracks. Halfway out of the garden, one of the guards walked over and shouted for me to get back to work. I did as I was told. The guards and the man walked the rest of the way back to our quarters.

When the evening ended, and we were back to have our evening meal, I walked up to the man's bunk. He was moaning. I knew he was very sick and needed to go to a doctor. I knew this was impossible. I walked out to where the officers were eating their meal. I had carried a rag with me and I saw a bucket of water. I put the rag in the water and went back to the barracks and quickly began to wipe the face of the ill officer to cool him down. By now his eyes were rolled back in his head. I knew he wouldn't last very long. The poor man was so sick. There was no medication for him. One of the guards walked in and yelled for me to get out and to go eat with the other men. I was so angry. I felt so bad that I couldn't even wipe his head and face. I pushed the rice and monias around on my plate—I couldn't even eat. I pretended to eat and, when the men finished their food, we walked back to the barracks. No one was in the room except us officers. I walked up to the sick officer and he was still moaning. I walked to the faucet in the back. I carried my towel with me and ran water all over it. I quickly walked back inside and I began to wipe the officer's face. I kept cooling him off for a long time. It wasn't helping. I felt someone's hand on my back. It was the chaplain. I knew he was praying. He was so gentle with him. He was talking softly. All at once the officer stopped moaning the way he had been. He took a deep breath, and was gone.

I looked at the chaplain. "Can't you do something?" He looked at me and said that there was nothing he could do. "He is gone now," he said. I looked at the chaplain with tears in my eyes. I noticed tears in his, as well. Such sadness. Death is never easy to take. At least he wouldn't suffer anymore. Oh, how awful to see someone suffer the way this officer did. I felt like I was going out of my mind. Oh, how I hated the Vietcong! Such a tragedy happening now, and so many over the years.

I felt a hand on my shoulder. "It's okay. You will get over this. You will be free one day. Hold on a little longer," he softly whispered to me.

I hated these words—hold on a little longer. We'd all held on a little longer and where did it get us? I kept these feelings tucked in my head.

The chaplain walked over to his bunk. I could see his head was bowed. I assumed he was praying. The guards came in to pick up the body. I looked away. I couldn't face seeing them taking him out.

As the days passed, following the death of the officer, I suddenly remembered the day his wife came to visit him. She had brought their son with her. Did they realize that visit would be the last time they would see him alive?

I walked around for several days just sort of living. I went about my duties but nothing else.

My father and one of my brothers came to visit me. I was glad to see them. I was glad that my mother was not with them. I loved her very much, but I don't think at this particular time I could face seeing her cry. She always had such a hurt in her eyes when they would leave. My brother did most of the talking about what he and his family were doing. We chatted for a while before it was time to leave. That evening, the guard brought in a package that my mother had sent. She had sent washcloths and towels. I really did need them.

Another prisoner fell in the garden. I hoped he would get better soon. I thought he got overheated. I didn't think I could go through another death so soon after the one we'd lost a few days ago.

Today we got a shave and a haircut. Most of us had lice that we couldn't seem to get rid of. We all lived in such close quarters and nothing was kept as clean as we would have liked.

When the rainy season came around again, I knew we had been here one year. So much happened in that one year. We had completed one garden and started on another. We had moved again, our third time since moving to the South. We never moved far away from one place to another. I still did not know why we moved so often. None of us was in any kind of condition to be traveling on foot. It didn't matter what our thoughts were. We did as we were told.

I lost another tooth—the fourth one. I kept brushing my teeth, trying to save what I had left. My knees, as usual, were my main concern. They hurt so badly. I could hardly move anymore.

One night, I dreamed that I was back at one of the bases in Texas. A doctor walked in and stuck a needle in my knees and fluid kept coming out. When I awoke, I thought this had actually happened. When I got out of my bunk, my knees could barely hold me up. My dream had seemed so real. I wished it had been.

Each day, we worked in the garden. Once in a while during the rainy season, we couldn't go out to work because of all the mud. I always liked to work, even if I hurt, because being kept inside was so depressing.

Every month or so we continued to have someone die. Most of them died from a medical problem or from a lack of food. For years now we only had enough food to keep us alive. Had it not been for the packages of food from our families, we would have had more die than we did.

Another year passed; this added up to nine years wasted, from not being home with my family.

Again the work days never varied. Working in the garden and feeling exhausted even before we began, eating the little food, and falling into bed, only to experience the same horrible dreams. These were our lives.

The men in my group were down to about 30. We had been together all these years. We no longer received mail because our families were nearby. We still had the old mail—we read over them for lack of anything else to do. The letters were old and dirty and barely legible. They were still precious to us just the same.

I wished the days flew by but they didn't. The days were long and tiring. The only time it flew by was at nighttime. When we got up in the morning it seemed as if we had just bedded down. We didn't sleep very well because of the devastatingly morbid dreams we had. When we woke up from having them, it would be a long time before we could drift off again.

My wife and children came to see me. Oh, my children were growing up much too fast. Hieu had gotten tall and gangly. I guess it was because of his age. He was a teenager now. My girls were both pretty like their mother. My wife was so beautiful that I would have a hard time catching my breath when she would sit down at the table. I was getting older and I knew I looked terrible to her. She never seemed to look older. She was more beautiful now than when we first married. I felt so lucky to have her and our children.

One of the men had left the quarters the day before. I don't think he'd died. He was a lower rank than me. I hoped he did well. I began to notice that a few were leaving and each one was a lower rank. There was never any kind of fanfare when we noticed they were no longer with us. We could never be sure why they left. Oh, God. I wished I would be going home.

The men who tried to get us to join the Communist Party were still coming around. I supposed they were still hopeful. We still sat up straight when they came. We listened to all of their promises. We would do like always and try to hold on until we could be released.

My father and one of my brothers came to see me one morning. I was called from the garden where I was working. The guard told us we had 10 minutes as we all sat around the table. My father looked older than the last time that I saw him. It literally broke my heart to see him age before my eyes. It was so good to see them. Like the last time that he came, my brother did most of the talking about plans he had been working on. I was thrilled for him. The guard jumped up and informed us that our time was up. I thanked them for coming and they left. I walked back to the garden to resume my work. I felt optimistic that the guard would bring me a sack that my father and brother had left. I hoped that they would not take too much out of the sack for themselves.

Later that evening one of the guards brought the sack to me. There was some food, which I was more than thankful to get, plus a small jar of salve for my knees. I shared the food with my fellow officers nearby.

At bedtime, I spread the salve all over my knees. I could feel a warm sensation and I hoped it would help.

The days and weeks sort of ran together. Our families came to visit and left much too soon. Our work in the garden never let up. The prisoners were still eating the earthworms from the soil. I no longer looked at it as strange. They were hungry and if the worms helped to keep them alive then that is what they should do.

CHAPTER FIVE

RELEASED FROM PRISON, 1984, AGE 42

One day, while we were working out in the garden, a guard walked out and began telling several of us to go into the compound. We all walked inside where a meeting was being held. An agent was standing in front of us with a list of names that he began to call out. I heard my name called. He told us we were being released. Those whose names were not called were told to go back to the garden. We were all in shock.

We were told to go to our bunks and collect our belongings. One of the guards handed me a box to put mine in.

A truck was waiting. The guard told me to get inside. Before the driver took off, the guard told me, "You can still come back at any time if you don't obey the rules! You will have to go to the Security Office to sign papers every month. They will tell you what to do."

My heart was beating so fast that I thought I would have a heart attack! I closed the door and the driver took off. I did exactly what I did 10 years ago when I was captured—I never looked right or left. My knees were shaking and I noticed so was my box. I tried so hard to keep still.

I tried to act as if this were an everyday occurrence. I hoped the guard didn't see my box shaking—I didn't want to give him the satisfaction of seeing me so scared.

After we rode for a few miles, the driver stopped the truck and told me to get out. "You will walk the rest of the way," he said. I quickly got out and closed the door. The driver turned around and went back the way he had come. I began walking. After a while the box seemed to get heavier. I was shaking something awful. I kept repeating to myself, "I'm going home. I'm going home. I'm free."

I walked a few miles and a man on a motor scooter drove by and stopped. We looked at each other. "You need a ride?" he inquired. I told him, "Yes," and he said, "Get on the back." He then asked me where I was going and I had to think very fast. My parents lived closer than my wife's parents; I quickly gave him the address and we took off. We must have made an unusual pair! I was dirty, I had no shoes, and I was carrying a box that I desperately tried to hang on to. I kept thinking at any moment I was going to lose it.

When we reached my parents' house, I told the man how much I appreciated the ride. He wished me luck and took off.

I looked up at my parents' house. Everything was so quiet. I walked up to the door and knocked. My mother opened the door, took one look at me, and closed the door.

"Mother, it's me. Let me in—I'm your son!"

She opened the door for me. "I thought you were a vagrant!" She grabbed me and helped me inside. She began to cry, "What have they done to you? You don't even look like my son!" I told her that I was let go from the prison.

Inside, I let the box fall to the floor. I stumbled into the room that I had shared with my brothers so many years before. I fell on the bed. I must have slept for hours. When I walked out of the room, my mother heard me—she told me that I needed a bath. She quickly had one ready in no time. I peeled off the old uniform or what was left of it. My mother put the filthy ragged clothes into a sack. I suppose she threw them into the trash.

Oh, how wonderful it was to ease down into the tub. This was my very first bath I'd had in 10 years. I scrubbed myself and washed my hair. After I dried myself, my mother set out some clothing that had belonged to one of my brothers. I quickly put them on. They hung on my body. I didn't care. Not only was this my first real bath but these were my first real clothes that I'd had in 10 years!

As I walked into the front room, I met my father coming in through the front door. He was shocked to see me. We embraced. I guess I looked different. I had lost so much weight. I told him I was let out of prison. He was so glad to see me! My mother had prepared the evening meal. I sat down at the table. The smell of the food was making me sick. I had not seen good clean food in so long. I took a couple of bites but I couldn't eat any more. My mother told me she understood.

Every once in a while I turned my body to look behind me. "What are you looking at, son?" my father asked.

I was so sorry. I hadn't noticed that I had been doing this. "I keep thinking one of the guards will rush up to me and shout to be quiet," I said. "This is the way we lived for the last 10 years."

I told my parents that I had to go to the Security Office and sign some papers. My father told me he would go there with me the next morning. I was so glad to be at home! I wished I could be with my wife and children—maybe I would be able to see them very soon. I asked my parents how my wife and children were doing. They told me they were all well and that they would be so surprised to see me! I also asked about my grandparents. Mother told me that all four of them had died while I was in prison. It made me so sad to hear this. They had all died before I was let out.

I couldn't sleep at bedtime. I tossed and turned all night. I was so excited to probably see my wife and children the next day.

The next morning, my father told me to use his razor so that I could shave. I lathered my face and looked in the mirror. I could hardly believe that the person who looked back at me was really me! My eyes had a look of shock and wildness about them. My hair was so thin with patches and stubbles here and there. My face was so thin. I looked nothing like my old self. I looked completely different from the young man who left here to begin my life as an airman all those many years ago. I began to shave and tears ran down my face into the lather, making streaks all down my face.

When I finished shaving, I thought I would look somewhat better, but instead, I looked at the old man looking back at me in the mirror. This was not me, I thought.

My mother had prepared some rice soup to eat for breakfast. I was surprised it stayed down. It tasted really good.

My father brought in a pair of old shoes and some socks for me to wear to the Security Office. I had not even thought about wearing shoes. It had been so long since I had shoes on my feet. I put them on at the door. It felt so strange. They felt like a foreign object on my feet.

We walked over to the Security Office. I signed my name and my father and I sat down to wait for my name to be called.

I learned I would have to come back once a month and have my release papers stamped. I was told that I could not hold down a job and I couldn't go anywhere without letting them know. I couldn't even go to my wife and children for a week. I was really angry, but I didn't let on. I had to be very careful about everything I did. There was nothing I could do but wait.

We walked back to my parents' house. I would find things to do to help them out. I certainly didn't want to go back to prison.

My father got word to my wife and she was told all about the rules that I was to follow. She was happy that I was out of prison and she could wait one week; after all, she had waited 10 years and a week was not that long. My wife was so patient. I wished I was more like her.

I found little jobs around the house to do to help my parents as much as I could. My knees had bothered me so much that I had to rest after a couple of hours. My mother rubbed my knees with ointment and put hot towels around them to ease the pain. This helped so much.

I missed my three brothers and sister so much. My brothers were all engineers and all of them were married except one who eventually became a monk. One brother was living in Australia with his family and one of his children was a doctor. My sister was married and she also had children. I would eventually see everyone—except the brother who lived in Australia. The days passed slowly and in some small way, I was happy to be with my folks to try to help them.

Finally, the day came to go back to the Security Office and sign more papers to let them know where I was going and the address where I would be. My father-in-law came to my parents' house to drive me to my wife. It was so good to see him again. I tried to tell him how much I appreciated all that he had done for my wife and children, but he would not let me say all that I wanted to say. He only said that he understood and then he smiled at me.

When we drove back up to the house, the children were at the door waiting for us. They hugged and kissed me. Then Lien walked into the room and the whole world stopped for me. I had to apologize for getting tears in my eyes. Everyone looked so healthy. My oldest, Hieu, seemed so shy but I knew he was glad to see me. He was 15 years old. My beautiful girls, Thao and Quyen, looked so much like their mother. Thao was now a teenager at 13 and Quyen was 10. We all sat down. The children kept looking at me. I felt so ashamed to be so awful looking. I hoped that in time they would be able to look past who they were looking at now. Lien and her mother had made a wonderful meal to welcome me home. Everyone gathered at the table and I hoped I could eat without feeling sick. I thanked them for going to so much trouble for me. I was able to take more than one bite of the delicious food. We all began to talk and at this time I felt like everyone was not focused on how I looked.

After dinner, Lien and her mother began to clean the kitchen. My father-in-law and I stayed seated as he wanted to fill me in on the news around town. Out of the corner of my eye, I could see Quyen easing herself next to me. I put my arm around her and it was all I could do to not start crying again. I did not want to frighten her. All at once, Thao was beside her sister and I put my arm around her too. I felt so blessed to finally be home. There was so much time to make up. I made a decision right then that even though I had missed out on everything for the last 10 years, I could go forward and be the best father and husband I could be. There was no way I could make up for those lost years; I could only look to the years to come.

That evening, when we all went to bed, I finally dozed off only to wake up moaning. I was deep in sleep with the horrible dream that had plagued me every night for the last 10 years. Lien comforted me. I felt so ashamed for disturbing her. She assured me it was all right and finally I went to sleep.

The next day, I told Lien's father to find me something to do around the house. I told him that I could not sit around day after day without something to occupy my mind. In time, between the two of us, we found plenty to keep me busy with—things that would make me feel as if I was contributing my share to help out. Every once in a while, I found myself wanting to fall into depression. I would quickly tell myself to not go there. I had only to tell myself of how it was before.

In the weeks to come, I started to put on a pound or two. My hair began to fill in where I had bald spots. My knees still bothered me but not to the extent that they used to be. I was so thankful for this.

The one thing I missed in prison, besides my family and good clean food, was having a bath. I enjoyed my daily bath at my in-laws' house so much. Lien couldn't get over how dirty the heels of my feet were. Each day she would soak my feet and then scrub them trying to get rid of all the years of walking barefoot in mud. This went on for a long time until finally my heels were normal once again.

I stayed busy helping out around the house and tending to the garden I had started right after I returned to my family. This would be the first time in 10 years—although I worked in the many gardens in prison—that I could finally get to reap the harvest!

I was still going to the Security Office each month to have them stamp my papers. Going there was something I never felt comfortable doing.

The children were growing daily and doing well in school. I couldn't ask any more than this. One year passed and then another. Hieu was 17 years old at this time and it was difficult to think he was about my age when I began thinking about joining the Air Force.

My health was the best I had been in since before prison. I had gained the few pounds I had lost, and I certainly felt better. My horrible dreams that I had in prison still came around nightly. Lien always calmed me down afterward. I had hoped at some point they would stop, but for now I had to contend with them.

I saw as many of my buddies as I could over the years. Every once in a while I would hear of one being released and it was so nice to be able to visit. We never talked about prison because it was too difficult. We talked about our families mostly and, like I had predicted, we were like family.

My wife and family told me to try to forget all that had happened. This was difficult to do. Sometimes I couldn't help but think about the past. It was a large chunk of my life. I didn't talk to the family about certain things because it made them so sad.

I thought about all of the trials we had been through while in prison. My health—along with the health of the other officers—which was almost taken away. The teeth I had lost. The pain I had endured with my knees. The hard labor over the years and those who had died unnecessarily after years of trying to hang on. Being so hungry that some ate earthworms to stay alive. All the many years away from our wives and children and the children growing up without a father's guidance. Those many times we endured the slow and painful deaths of the officers tied to trees. All of those wasted years hoping to be released to finally go home. Then, if this was not enough, because of the war, many changes happened, and one that hurt me probably more than anything was to lose my retirement from being a Major in the Air Force. Yes, I'll admit that the Vietcong took away so much of ourselves, but they couldn't take away our dignity. I'm very proud to say this.

I often thought about the good years I spent in training in Texas and Louisiana and the many times playing table tennis. I thought about the many friends I encountered along the way and the trip to Washington, D.C. with my three buddies. All of these memories were pleasant and I liked to replay them in my mind.

Time went by and we were still at my in-laws' house. Hieu graduated from high school and the girls were growing fast. I still went to the Security Office monthly and I hated each time I had to go.

Going to Live in the United States

One day a beautiful thing happened. The United States Government informed the Vietnamese Government that all of the officers who were in the Communist Prison Camp for three years or more would be able to go to the United States to live and become American citizens. (We still to this day don't know exactly how all of that was done; after all, my country was now Communist. But it did happen and I'm thankful that it did!)

This was a dream come true! None of us could believe it! I filled out an application for myself, my wife, and children who were also included. After I did all of the necessary paperwork, we had to wait until everything was approved. Finally everything was accepted and approved. Now we had to wait until we could actually leave.

In January, 1990, we received word that my family and I could at last leave Vietnam. A Catholic organization called U.S.C.C. would sponsor us and they would pay all of our expenses.

We would be leaving family members, which was sad to do, but all of them were very pleased that we had this wonderful opportunity to get to live in a free country.

My parents had both died two years prior to us leaving. This was an emotional time for us. They had sacrificed so much for their children and I have only wonderful memories of them. I will always be grateful to have had them for my parents.

Coming to America

When I filled out the papers to come to the US, I chose Houston, Texas to live because my brother, Hai, who was an engineer and now a monk, lived there. Plus my wife's sister and her husband, who is a doctor, also lived in the Houston area.

We were leaving Vietnam with bitter feelings. There were so many hurts we would be leaving and so many deaths of my own people during the war; also so many deaths of the American troops who lost their lives trying to help save our South Vietnam from Communism.

Now we were going to a beautiful country that was free and we would leave with as many hopes and dreams.

We arrived in Houston December 16, 1991 and the U.S.C.C. organization folks met us at the airport. They had found us a place to live for the time being. They drove us there to get settled. They were so caring and thoughtful. We were told that we needed to go to the Social Security Office before we made any big decisions. They told us that the U.S.C.C. folks would be with us the next morning to take us there.

We learned so much information at the Social Security Office.

Everyone in my family would receive $200 monthly for one year plus we would receive Medicaid, which would cover the cost of any medical needs. Also for one year, we would receive food stamps. What a wonderful opportunity! I would do everything in my power to accept these graciously and with great gratitude. This would have never happened in the country we had just left. There were no words to express how grateful we were for this generosity.

Our home had all of the necessities and now we needed to enroll our youngest in high school, and ESL classes for the other two. We wanted to make sure our children learned the language.

I found a part-time job at a laundromat. My hours were 2:00 a.m–10:00 a.m. They were not ideal hours but I was not choosey. It was a job and I would be the best that I could be. I had to make sure that the machines were in working order and that the place was kept clean. I was at this job for four months and I found another job as a cashier at a Shell gas station. I loved meeting new people—the hours were good and the pay was better. I worked there four years. Then I got another job working for a Medical Supply Company.

The families we lived around found out that Lien could sew beautifully. In no time, she had many customers from all over the Houston area.

I was able to repay the money that the Catholic Organization gave us to come to Houston. It wasn't something I had to do, but it was the right thing to do. With our food stamps we made sure that we didn't abuse them. We bought only what we needed.

In the years 1998 to 1999 our family of five became American Citizens. What a wonderful feeling to really belong here and truly be Americans!

Today I am 75 years old. As I reflect on my life, so many things have happened in those years.

During the war, the American troops worked so diligently to help us. During their years in the war, they lost so much. It is reported that they lost 58,200 troops who were killed or missing in action. So many returned home wounded.

Our children speak English very well. They are all married and Lien and I have nine grandchildren. One grandson has almost completed University and the others, no doubt, will follow. We are proud of them all!

Every few years, the officers who were in prison have a reunion. We are all scattered across the US. In the Houston area, I'm proud to say, we see each other often. We are all close, as I had predicted. The Chaplain, Su Nghi, who played such a big part in all of our lives in prison, is in his eighties now. He is still active in his Baptist Church along with his family. It's always a joy to see and visit with him.

My family has done very well since we became citizens. Our children own their homes as well as my wife and me. Our family owns our business and we have been very successful. We have worked very hard to achieve the American dream.

Every morning when I wake up, I am happy to be where we are in this beautiful country that is free. It has given my family so much and because of this, much is required from us. I will always be thankful for all we have. I'm happy to say that I am free of those horrible dreams I once had. They, like everything else, are in the past. I look forward to the good years to come.

My grandchildren have no idea what I have gone through, even though they think they do. I'm hoping this book will enlighten them and cause them to be better Americans.

ACKNOWLEDGMENTS

First and foremost, I would like to thank Thanh Chau for giving me this story. It is a story that needed to be told, and I am proud to be chosen to write it.

I would like to thank my husband, Ed, for his encouragement and for the many hours he lovingly endured while I was left alone to write.

To my children, Portland and Stephen, and your spouses, for listening patiently to parts of the story as I read them aloud to you on numerous occasions! I love you dearly!

To my sweet cousin Dorothy, for your encouragement and love during these many years.

To my cousins in South Carolina—Cousin Hud and Cousin Mittie. Your sweet words were enduring.

To my grandchildren, who thought Mi Mi was never going to finish this book. Thank you for being my sweet babies, even though you are all grown and most have completed college.

To my four great grandbabies, I love each one and I pray each one will have a love for books.

To my sister, Lou, I thank you for listening long distance to any new page that I had written. Thank you.

To my brother, Bill, whose words of encouragement meant so much. Thank you.

To my best friends, Pat and Jerry Vavra, who heard all about this book while we were eating at each other's home. I had a captive audience, so you patiently listened! Thanks so much!

To my special friends, Tim and Patricia O'Grady, thank you for telling me how good you thought the book would be, especially at a time when I was bogged down. Your sweet words meant so much.

To my sweet Pastor Neil and family at GPBC, for your special love for our family.

To my Bible study teacher on Sunday mornings, Tommy Hamor. Thank you for teaching me so much about the Bible. Thank you, friend, for your words of encouragement.

To the three principals that I especially loved at Kennedy Elementary: *Betty Best*—the first principal at Kennedy. You were a joy to work under and even to this day I can call you my friend. Thanks for the times we can get together. *Lily Beth Wilson*—Thank you for your words of wisdom. It's always a pleasure when we see each other. *Mary Hoskings*—Thank you for your words of encouragement and for all of the sweet notes you wrote and put in my box at school. They were priceless!

To Helen Mata, my first ESL teacher that I worked with. You taught me the true meaning of love. Thank you for the wonderful memories that I will always treasure.

To Pat Cady, one of the most intelligent people I have ever known! You taught me so much in ESL. You are a true friend!

To my sweet cousin Marjorie Bailey, thank you for being so special all of these years. Thank you for always asking how the book was coming; your words of encouragement kept me going.

To Kathryn Quackenbush—Your first words to me were always, "Have you finished the book?" Thank you for being that special cousin!

To my English teacher in Calvert High School, Loma Brannon (deceased). You taught me well. You were the first one to tell me I had a flair for writing. I think of you often with fond memories.

To Nikki Dang, thank you for your love and words of encouragement.

To Barbara Chrisman, thank you for all of your help with this book. Your prayers and words of encouragement meant so much to me.

Last but not least, thank you to my Heavenly Father for giving me this creative mind!

2011 at wedding party
I was 69 years old.

At my home town in
Thuận Hưng village. This time
I just released from communist
camp in 1985. I was
43 years old.

I was 22 years old, when I
graduated at Randolph A.F.B on T-28
at September 1964.

95 geo. Eng. AFB

AD-6 Skyraider 1967
1500

I got around 3,000 flying hours